Helping Children and Adolescents Think about Death, Dying and Bereavement

of related interest

Communicating with Children When a Parent is at the End of Life
Rachel Fearnley
ISBN 978 1 84905 234 4
eISBN 978 0 85700 475 8

Talking About Death and Bereavement in School
How to Help Children Aged 4 to 11 to Feel Supported and Understood
Ann Chadwick
ISBN 978 1 84905 246 7
eISBN 978 0 85700 527 4

Great Answers to Difficult Questions about Death
What Children Need to Know
Linda Goldman
ISBN 978 1 84905 805 6
eISBN 978 1 84642 957 6

Seeds of Hope Bereavement and Loss Activity Book
Helping Children and Young People Cope with Change Through Nature
Caroline Jay
Illustrated by Unity-Joy Dale
ISBN 978 1 84905 546 8
eISBN 978 0 85700 970 8

What Does Dead Mean?
A Book for Young Children to Help Explain Death and Dying
Caroline Jay and Jenni Thomas
Illustrated by Unity-Joy Dale
ISBN 978 1 84905 355 6
eISBN 978 0 85700 705 6

A Sky of Diamonds
A Story for Children About Loss, Grief and Hope
Camille Gibbs
ISBN 978 1 84905 622 9
eISBN 978 1 78450 093 1

Helping Children and Adolescents Think about Death, Dying and Bereavement

Marian Carter

Jessica Kingsley *Publishers*
London and Philadelphia

All Bible quotations are taken from the New Revised Standard Version Bible: Anglicized Edition, copyright 1989, 1995, Division of Christian Education of the National Council of the Churches of Christ in the United States of America. Used by permission. All rights reserved.

First published in 2016
by Jessica Kingsley Publishers
73 Collier Street
London N1 9BE, UK
and
400 Market Street, Suite 400
Philadelphia, PA 19106, USA

www.jkp.com

Copyright © Marian Carter 2016

Printed digitally since 2016

Library of Congress Cataloging in Publication Data
Names: Carter, Marian, author. Title: Helping children and adolescents think about death, dying, and
bereavement / Marian Carter. Description: Philadelphia : Jessica Kingsley Publishers, 2016. | Includes
bibliographical references and index. Identifiers: LCCN 2016004457 | ISBN 9781785920110 (alk. paper) Subjects: LCSH: Children and death. | Death--Psychological aspects. Classification: LCC BF723.D3 C37 2016 | DDC 155.9/37083--dc23 LC record available at https://lccn.loc.gov/2016004457

British Library Cataloguing in Publication Data
A CIP catalogue record for this book is available from the British Library

ISBN 978 1 78592 011 0
eISBN 978 1 78450 255 3

*To all the children who have challenged
me and from whom I have learnt.*

To Jo Roberts, a friend and encourager.

*To editors Natalie Watson, Jane Evans and
Kerrie Morton for their wise and helpful comments.*

Contents

Introduction

Working in schools, hospitals, hospices and a parish I have been challenged and inspired by the insights from and conversations with children and young people. It is an amazing privilege. I have always been a teacher in primary and secondary schools and trained teachers and clergy while working throughout in a voluntary capacity with children and adolescents. Bereavement has been a significant area of conversations. For nine months, I lived with a family whose young mother had died leaving three children and learnt rapidly the understandings and needs of each of them. More recently, I have been alongside my teenage niece, an only child, in the terminal illness and death of my sister, her mother. I have worked in a hospital with responsibility as a chaplain for the Special Care Baby Unit; then as a full-time hospice chaplain I was involved with the children and grandchildren of patients, leading funerals with children present and running courses for teachers and social workers on bereavement care.

The book is concerned with how children and adolescents understand death, their own mortality and the death of someone they love, including pets; how children deal with bereavement and funerals; and how they can be supported in continuing care. It is intended to be used by parents and professionals, children and youth workers, health professionals, social workers, funeral directors, teachers and ministers of religion – both those in training and qualified in all these professions – who face children's grief and their questions about death.

This is a theoretical and practical resource, since there is no comprehensive book available, and this is a growing concern with the recognition that learning about death is part of a child's 'primary socialisation' without which the child is likely, subsequently through adult life, to suffer psychological problems such as depression when faced with mortality. I have experienced that children have a freshness and openness in attitudes to death and can be a model from which adults can learn; adolescents are more thought-provoking! The examples in this book are from my own experience (the names have been changed to honour confidentiality). Although most of my experience is from a UK perspective, research indicates and includes North American perspectives.

Since this book is significant as a resource for those who do not have faith, the material on faiths will be with a light touch. Children do ask questions about death such as, 'Where is granny now?' We need to be open in exploring these with children. These are questions common to those of different religious faiths, and those with none.

Each chapter has a pattern beginning with an illustrative diagram – the hermeneutical circle (see below) – since it begins with experience and leads finally to practical responses. At times, I refer back to the original experience: this is an example of the 'spiral curriculum', since when we return we will have a deeper understanding of a situation.

Each chapter also includes activities to elicit the reader's experience.

Chapter overview

Chapter 1: What is Death?

Children suffer losses, and death is the ultimate loss. Death is experienced in many ways – on the TV news, children playing 'dead' in the playground or the death of someone close, for example a parent, grandparent, favourite teacher or sibling. The development of the stages of understanding in children come from insights in the psychological and social sciences and listening to the experience of children's voices and questions. Both those of faith and those with none wrestle with the meaning and significance of death.

Chapter 2: Grief and Bereavement

Children experience a range of emotions and express their grief in related behaviour. Grief may seem like jumping in and out of puddles, one minute sobbing the next asking what is for tea. Adolescent grief is more hidden. The grief of an adult is more consistent and is often hidden, a taboo in UK culture. World faiths have rituals and customs of grieving which are distinctive to each faith.

Chapter 3: Challenging Factors Influencing Grief

Grief and the behaviours associated with it depend on the nature of the relationship. Each person responds in their own way. Grief is unique. Different types of death are explored – a miscarriage, terminal illness of a child and parent, a sudden death and a suicide. Each bereavement is unique.

Chapter 4: What Should We Tell Children and Adolescents?

As adults we need to listen to the child; children are very realistic and 'down to earth'. This listening will give us clues to the approach to use to comfort and reassure children. Euphemisms such as 'Gran has gone away for a holiday' and 'Grandad is a star in the sky' are examined. Anticipatory grief and actual grief raise questions about how much a child should be told about a situation. Adolescents need listening to rather than telling. World faiths explore understandings of a life beyond death. How is this handled with children? Is it possible to live on beyond death?

Chapter 5: Schools Coping with Bereavement and Death

Bereaved and grieving children and young people attend school. Should schools respond? An exploration of response is through the significance and practice of pastoral care and through the curriculum.

Models of these two responses are suggested. A large proportion of schools are faith schools and reflect each of the different world faiths. Their contribution and the criticism of them are examined.

Chapter 6: Funerals: The Attendance and Participation of Children and Adolescents

Should children be encouraged to attend a funeral? We look at preparing a child for what will happen at a funeral. Can a funeral be child friendly? What arrangements need to be made for a child or adolescent to attend a funeral? Can a child play a role in the funeral? What are the alternatives, if we are taking grief in a child or adolescent seriously? The rituals of each of the world faiths are examined.

Chapter 7: Continuing Care of Children and Adolescents

What form might this take and who might be responsible? As adults we sometimes forget that a child or adolescent needs to revisit a significant loss. However, the continuing remembrance of a loss may become pathological and need professional help. There are public occasions when those who have died are remembered, such as at the Cenotaph. Practical suggestions are given in the chapter to help children and adolescents positively to grieve.

Chapter 8: Care of the Carers Including Ourselves

Parents and professionals are asked to recognise their own losses and remember how they coped; these losses might well be ignited again in working with bereaved children and adolescents. Resources for 'stress busting' are examined and spiritual resources are also looked at.

Chapter 9: Weaving the Threads Together

This chapter is a summary of the important points in regard to the care of bereaved children and adolescents including how, as adults, we can learn from them as well as responding to their grief and distress.

The methodology used in this book

I have attempted to use the methods of Paulo Freire (1921–1997), so that as a reader you may make links with your own professional experience and relate new insights to your existing life experience and knowledge. Paulo Freire challenged traditional education methods in his book *Pedagogy of the Oppressed*. His emphasis was on dialogue signifying respect in the pupil–teacher relationship, in contrast to what he describes as the 'banking' type of education, where the educator 'deposits' knowledge into the mind of the listener or reader. Freire believed that the educator had to forget himself, to die in order to be born again and to educate alongside, to teach and learn from the person being taught. Education was about praxis; it deepened understanding and made a difference to building community, leading to actions for justice and human flourishing. His is a pedagogy of hope. He wrote of conscientisation, of developing a consciousness in people that has the power to transform their thinking and attitudes. Freire's learning used personal experience, narrative, the senses, the imagination, life stories, experience and exploring together. I have attempted to follow his example.

The method to be used in this book is one of lifelong learning. In current adult education individuals are encouraged to have a 'buddy' or a 'mentor'. The invitation is for the reader to find someone with whom to share. You will be invited to engage with this book through activities, questions and reflection in the section of each chapter headed 'Activities to elicit the reader's experience'. My hope is that you and your 'work' in supporting bereaved children and adolescents will be enriched. If you would like to enter into a more personal dialogue, then that is possible. I have set up a website (dyingtolive.org.uk) for conversations and comments.

1

What is Death?

If you never get born you never have to die, but you miss a lot.
(Alison in Marshall 2003, p.86)

A child's experience

Stephanie, a three-year-old, lived in a rural village. She and her mother came across a dead pheasant while walking across a field. Stephanie was rather surprised that it did not seem to move. Her mother explained that it was dead. 'If I breathe on it, will it come alive?' she asked. Later Stephanie asked her mother, 'Will you die, Mummy?' 'One day,' her mother replied, 'but when you are much older.'

Reflection on experience

We each have a need to make meaning from our experiences of life. Children have a drive to make sense of the world in which they live and Stephanie was doing just that. She knew that living things like pheasants move and breathe; if she breathed on the pheasant, it might live. Early humans noted the importance of the breath. The breath was the life, the spirit of a person. When the breath ceased, so did life and death resulted. Children need their questions answered honestly. Her question, 'Will you die, mummy?' needed the truthful answer, 'One day' and the reassuring words, 'but when you are much older' that her mother would be present for her now and for years to come.

An adolescent's experience

The major event of 11 September 2001 shook the world. Many people can recall where they were when the attack on the twin towers of the World Trade Center in New York City happened. Regular television and radio programmes were suddenly interrupted, and American TV took over. We watched in horror. Was this a film or reality? On a clear Tuesday morning an American Airlines Boeing 767 with passengers on board was hijacked and crashed in the North Tower leaving a gaping, burning hole near the 89th floor of the 110-storey skyscraper, instantly killing hundreds and trapping hundreds more in upper floors.

Eighteen minutes later a second Boeing 767 United Airlines Flight 175 turned sharply and sliced into the south tower near the 60th floor. Debris was showered over surrounding buildings. Fifteen minutes later the South Tower collapsed, followed later by the North Tower. Three thousand died in the World Trade Center and its vicinity, including 343 firefighters and paramedics, 23 police and 37 Port Authority police. The event dominated the news for several days. A year later a group of secondary school pupils in the UK were asked to recall the event. Natalie, aged 15, said:

> It was like something you saw in a film, but this was real, and that shook me up inside…I kept asking myself, how can any human being treat another with no care at all? No care about whether they live or die, no care about how many families they destroy. (Natalie, quoted in Duffy 2008, p.46)

Reflection on experience

We live in a world where communication can be almost instantaneous. Acts of terrorism continue, fear of further threats of death lie at the door. We are all involved. It may seem as Natalie said, at first like 'a film', but death is a reality, its presence and immanence unknown to us.

Linking adult, child and adolescent experience

In the UK, there is a taboo among adults about talking of death, but this is beginning to change. Groups like the Dying Matters Coalition are beginning to develop, and there are 'Death Cafes': the first in Britain took place in September 2011, organised by Jon Underwood, 'to create an environment where talking about death is natural and comfortable...death is a catalyst to think about important things in life' (Battersby 2012). Underwood mentions that we 'out-source' death to hospitals, behind closed doors, but gradually death is being brought out of the shadows (Battersby 2012). There are websites to be found on the internet through which you can find death cafes near you. Funeral festivals are advertised in national newspapers. They are organised by funeral directors concerned that people should know the choices of prepayment funeral plans, wills and advanced directives. In the USA, 'Death over Dinner' is encouraged as a way to talk in an informal way over a meal with friends and strangers about personal experiences with life and death. One hostess, a former hospice volunteer, said:

> We want to talk in an informal way about personal experiences with death. How do people want to die? Have you shared that with anyone? What deaths have you experienced? We don't want to be distasteful, or uncomfortable, but an uplifting atmosphere. (Hafiz 2013)

There are published accounts of dying such as those of *The Guardian* columnist John Diamond (Diamond 1998), Philip Gould (Gould 2012) and Christopher Hitchens (Hitchens 2012). There are guides to dying well, for example that by Rabbi Julia Neuberger (Neuberger 1999) and other factual and fiction books about death (Albom 2003; De Hennezel 1997; Levine 1986; Reoch 1997; Schwartz 1998). An online search will find 'training and life coaching classes' and one of the tasks on such a course is to write your obituary. This is a reality check to ask the questions 'why am I here?' and 'what do I want to be able to say about my life at the end?' In the USA, Legacy.com publishes self-written obituaries each month; the UK equivalent is ObitKit.com.

There have been reality type films such as the documentary *Life Before Death* (2002) about pain relief for dying patients, *Shadowlands* (1993) the story of C.S. Lewis's wife's dying, *Dying Young* (1991) about a nurse working with a dying young man, *I Didn't Want That* (2012), *The Bucket List – Time to Start Living* (2007) where two terminally ill men fulfil dreams before death and *The Fault in Our Stars* (2014), which tells the story of two teenage cancer patients beginning a life affirming journey. There have also been fantasy films such as *Death Becomes Her* (1992) where an immortality treatment replaces death, *Sixth Sense* (1999) in which a young man communes with spirits of the dead and *Lonely Bones* (2009), in which a murdered girl comes to visit her family. In the UK, the Wellcome Institute had a display from autumn 2012 to spring 2013: 'Death: A Self-Portrait, the Richard Harris Collection'. A newspaper stated:

> Death in a secular and medicalized world has been made into something to be put off. All credit to the Wellcome Foundation for holding a show that reminds us that death has been an intrinsic part of life through most of human history. (Hamilton 2012)

In contrast to an adult obsession, young children in particular are fascinated by death and talk about it naturally, though their concept development is different from that of adults. The American psychologist J.A. Graham believes that children's comprehension of death depends on both experience and developmental level:

> Children's experiences with death (i.e. actual experience and what they have been told about death) are critical to their understanding, they also do not have enough life experience to realize that death is inevitable for all living things. Children may not understand that death is permanent and that it cannot be 'fixed' or reversed. (Graham 2013)

Death is a loss – the ultimate loss – and is experienced by children and adolescents. In 2012 in the UK over 3000 babies died before their first birthday – for reasons ranging from preterm underweight birth, poor prenatal care, poverty, social inequality and abuse – and over 2000 children and young people died between the ages of one and nineteen. One in five deaths is of those between 15 and 19 years as a result of road accidents, risk-taking behaviour, poisoning and cancer (Wolfe *et al.* 2014).

Every day more than a hundred children in the UK are bereaved of a parent, 24,000 every year; 6 per cent of 5–16-year-olds – 537,450 in the UK – have experienced the death of a close friend of the family; and the incidence of memories of childhood bereavement undealt with in youth offenders can be up to ten times higher – 41 per cent – than the national average of 4 per cent. These facts and figures come from the charity Winston's Wish which is the major provider of care for the bereaved child in the UK.

Children and adolescents, in common with everyone, experience loss across a wide range of experience. Physical losses may be the security of the womb at birth, health through infections, a tooth, the hormonal change of puberty or an illness resulting in a loss of freedom which may be temporary or permanent. The ultimate loss is the death of a person – a grandparent, parent, sibling or peer-group friend – or a terminal illness of the child or adolescent himself. Social loss might include moving house and school through changed family circumstances with the ensuing break of friendship groups. Emotional loss is felt with the separation or divorce of parents, parents changing partners, the ending of a peer friendship and the breaking down of a relationship. A loss of self-esteem may result from poor marks in school, failing an important exam or parents' divorce. Loss can be spiritual loss, a feeling of being alone; a lack of self-worth; feeling unloved; or feeling life has no purpose. Loss can be vicarious through television dramas, 'soaps' and from adverts and computer games.

Sociological, psychological and historical insights

What is death? How is death historically defined? In 77–79 CE, the Roman author Pliny the Elder wrote in his *Historia Naturalis*, 'so uncertain is men's judgment that they cannot determine even death itself'. In 1768, the first edition of the *Encyclopaedia Britannica* defined death as, 'the separation of the soul and the body', reflecting the context of a predominantly religious society. In 1974, in the fifteenth edition of the *Encyclopaedia*, the definition was 30 times longer and solely from a biological standpoint. One reason for this is that medical advances make it more difficult to determine if a person is dead. The nearest definition is, 'the final cessation of activity in the central nervous system noted especially by a flat electroencephalogram for a predetermined length of time'. But is this satisfactory? Death can be 'reversed' with an electric shock, cardiopulmonary resuscitation (CPR). Breathing and heartbeat can sometimes be restarted. Without a functioning heart or lungs, life can be sustained with a combination of life support devices, organ transplants and artificial pacemakers.

The social historian Philippe Ariès notes changes in perceptions of death (Ariès 1974, p.28). He begins with 'tamed death', anticipated through natural signs and a dying person's premonition, typical of the Early Middle Ages. It needed preparation by the dying person: being at peace within one's self, making peace with others and God, so that the dying person could rest, knowing their immortality was assured. The Middle Ages emphasised humanity's collective judgement at the end of time, but by the fifteenth century the focus was on individual judgement after death, which called for preparation during life, and a manual emerged, *Ars Moriendi* (*Art of Dying*), to educate priests in ministry to the dying.

Today attitudes are very different. Ariès states that society denies death. It has become 'excluded, invisible, wild, untamed by ritual or community' (1981, p.585). Ariès believes this is related to the dominant model of western health care – the medical model – a sociological term which indicates that, from the mid-twentieth century, illnesses of body and mind have an underlying cause which can usually be diagnosed, removed, reversed or replaced in treatment. The patient is cured and can return to the status quo existing before the illness, thus death is denied. The success of medicine and public health can be seen in the figures of life expectancy in the UK, which rose from 44 years for males and 47 years for females in 1990 to 78.2 years for males and 82.3 years for females in 2012. However, if adults recognise and admit their mortality the prospect would become less fearful and adults might learn to enjoy the present moment.

A child or adolescent's knowledge of death

Knowledge of death today is extensive from seeing a dead bird or hedgehog in the road or garden, the death of a pet, a family member with a terminal illness (this might include the child or adolescent him or herself), witnessing a road accident, death reported in the media, films and game-stations. These death-related experiences in children are more common than adults realise. Understanding death is an important issue for children and begins at an early age.

The systematic study of children's understanding of death began in 1934 (Schilder and Wechsler 1934), and by 1995 there were over a hundred such studies in the English language. However, progress is slow and the results considered confusing (Speece 1995). Speece and Brent list reasons for the lack of progress and confusion; two of the most important appear to be first confusion over the names for, definitions of and operationalisations of the various aspects of the concept of death, and second, the lack of reliable and valid standardised measures for these aspects (Speece and Brent 1996). To help children we need to know how they think and how they process information; this is clarified by the research.

The categories below are guidelines only and should not be considered prescriptive for the child being helped. Children and adolescents mature at different rates and their understanding will depend on their life experience as much as their chronological age. It is important to remember that parents know their own child best. Children's and adolescents' concepts develop in stages from literal and concrete to abstract; this includes their concept of death which, since the 1970s, has been considered to be composed of several relatively distinct sub-concepts, referred to in the literature as 'components'. For most research four are cited: universality, irreversibility, non-functionality and causality.

Universality

This refers to the understanding that all living things must inevitably die. The younger the child, the more likely they are to say that death is not universal; some studies suggest children think that if you are clever, or lucky, death is avoidable; also that it happens to others, such as the old or the handicapped, but not to them (e.g. Speece 1995). It takes time before a young child extends death to himself.

Irreversibility

Once the physical body dies, it cannot be made alive again. Younger children are more likely to view death as temporary and reversible, similar to sleep from which a person wakes or a holiday from which there is a return. They may think reversal is possible as a result of wishful thinking, praying or medical intervention. The latter reflects advances in medical technology, but the success of cardiopulmonary resuscitation will depend on the availability of appropriate resources and the time factor of the nearness of medical help underlined by the changing definition of what constitutes 'alive' and 'dead'. In the research children also respond with non-corporeal responses. Common in young children is reference to 'heaven' although the issue of irreversibility is in reference to the physical body. Children, in common with many adults, often understand some form of personal continuation after the death of the physical body, a continuing of the soul or spirit without the body, or for others reincarnation in a new body.

Non-functionality

This refers to the understanding that at death all the life-determining capabilities of the physical – walking, eating, breathing, sensing – cease to function. Younger children are likely to think that the dead continue to be able to perform certain functions but not others. One researcher found that children are more likely to realise that concrete, observable functions such as eating and speaking cease with death, than recognise that internal functions such as thinking, dreaming and knowing cease.

Causality

There is no consensus on the definition of causality. Much research agrees that it involves an abstract and realistic understanding of the external and internal events that might possibly cause an individual's death, for example Speece (1995). 'Abstract' means that the given causes are not restricted to particular individuals or events but are classes of causes applicable to living things in general. 'Realistic' refers to the fact that the causes stated are generally accepted by mature adults as valid causes of death. Younger children may provide unrealistic causes related to themselves, such as bad behaviour, or specific concrete causes such as guns or accidents rather than more 'abstract' causes such as illness or old age. Young children lack understanding that death is finally a failure of internal body organs or functions.

Developmental stages and understanding of death

Younger children are likely to be more concrete in their thinking and understanding of death while the older child and adolescent are more realistic and abstract. The age at which children achieve an adult understanding of the four key components varies between four and twelve years. The majority of research suggests that at about seven years old most children have understood each of the four key bio-scientific components introduced above. Children are likely to 'revisit' any experience of death as they move through their developmental stages. I will return to how the conceptual stages influence behaviour and the care that needs to be taken with grieving children and bereaved adolescents in Chapter 2.

Babies do not understand that a parent, sibling or a close relative has died but sense the disappearance, particularly of someone who daily responded to their physical and emotional needs, and the feeling of sadness and the atmosphere of the home.

A toddler might show a basic understanding of death when he sees a dead bird or insect in the garden but does not usually understand the implications of this, for instance that the dead bird cannot feel anything or won't ever get up again. Toddlers continue to sense the emotional feelings of sadness or anxiety in the home when a significant person is missing and other relatives new to the child come into the house. Games like 'peek-a-boo' are loved by toddlers; in such games significant adults can disappear and reappear again and it is through these games that the child may slowly begin to understand the concept of 'gone for good'.

Three- to five-year-old preschool children are egocentric. Many consider that children of this age do not understand that death is final. Some psychologists disagree, believing that children can comprehend the permanence of death and can acquire a concept of heaven, albeit concrete, since they are literal thinkers – heaven is therefore somewhere with green fields, flowers, sunshine – whereas abstract concepts like 'forever' and the fact that death is permanent are difficult to grasp. They do not grasp that the functions of life have ceased – their questions reflect their concern about the physical wellbeing of the dead person. Children tend to think of death as like sleep or a journey: people wake up and Gran returns from holiday. Adults should not use the word 'sleep' or other euphemisms but the word death itself (see Chapter 4, 'What Should We Tell Children and Adolescents?'). A child may well ask about a dead mother, 'When will Mum be home?' Children use the word 'dead' without understanding its full meaning – Susie, a three-year-old, whose mother had died at home, was doing her jigsaw, but there was a piece missing. Susie said the piece was 'dead'. This age group is very matter of fact and ask questions which the adults may find difficult. They repeatedly want to know and be told the 'story' again. They are prone to magical thinking, experiencing themselves as the centre of life; they may believe that their thoughts or actions can cause things to happen to themselves and to others. The far-reaching consequences of a death are not yet apparent to them. Children of this age certainly express sadness and vividly describe their feelings, many describing this as physical pain.

Five- to nine-year-old children are concrete thinkers. At this stage children begin to develop an understanding that death is permanent and irreversible, with all life functions ended and final. They may be fascinated with the physical aspects of death or the rituals surrounding it. This derives from a developing imagination and 'magical thinking' and assumes a dead person can see and hear the living. It is an age of fear and fantasy. Children may personalise death as a skeleton, a monster or a ghost and may become curious about the rituals of death and functions of dead bodies, often asking if dead people need food or clothing, which reinforces the belief that their thoughts or actions caused the death and can lead them to fill in the gaps in their knowledge. A child may see death as a person who might 'come to get you' or 'catch you' if you are unlucky. This growing understanding can lead to a fear of going to sleep or of the dark. Children will need reassurance and comfort as they begin to realise their own mortality; something like a night light may be helpful.

By the age of seven, children seem to be able to appreciate that death is unavoidable and will happen to everyone, and that there is a concrete cause of death, such as old age or accident. At this age, generally, death means no longer being able to eat, sleep, laugh, cry or feel pain. All life functions have ended. They are reluctant to see death for themselves. Seven-year-old Amy's terminally ill mother died at home. Amy believed her mum died because the nurse was late in coming to care for her mum, not realising the death was due to the spread of her cancer. As they get older, children begin to have a more mature understanding of death, realising its 'external' causes – accidents – and 'internal, natural' causes such as disease and old age and that it is final, permanent, universal and an unavoidable part of life. Children can become fearful as a result of their deepening realisation of the possibility of their own future death.

Nine- to eleven-year-old children are generally very matter of fact, and the acceptance of death as a fact of life is evident. Death is accepted as finality for all living things. It is inevitable and irreversible. Their understanding of death is influenced by their own past experiences of death and dying and the explanations that were given to them at that time. There is a greater ability to think abstractly, with thinking about fairness and fate, justice and injustice in relation to life and death. These young people are aware that death will happen to them but do not wish to dwell on it, but get on with living. Some might continue to struggle with the finality of death possibly because of certain religious beliefs, states Graham (2013), a clinical psychologist in the USA. However, this may suggest a more mature understanding of death rather than a less mature one. Children with immature, binary concepts of death see people as either alive or dead, and do not consider the idea that there may be any other options based on religious values and ideas about an afterlife.

Adolescent understanding is influenced by the hormonal changes of the age group. This is a period when there is a search for identity and meaning in life and maturing cognitive ability. There is a gradual ability to comprehend the finality and enduring consequences of a loss coupled with the capacity to use abstract ideas and project the impact of a death of someone known to them, family or friend, to the future. Adolescents increasingly develop their own beliefs and strongly held views, and may challenge the beliefs and explanations offered by others. They sometimes find it hard to ask for support at a significant loss, trying to show the world they are independent. Adolescents may talk at length about the death, but seldom to those closest to them in the family. Their peer group are very significant at this time as a 'sounding board' distinct from the emotions of the family. The awareness of their own mortality may however show itself through risk-taking behaviour – 'dicing with death'– such as drug taking or racing at speed on a motorbike or in cars. Other characteristics are mood swings and a refusal to cooperate at home. There is interesting evidence relating to risk taking in adolescence. In some ways, this can be thought of as natural for adolescents who are kicking over the traces and establishing their own identities as distinct from that of their family and upbringing. Nevertheless, each activity involves high risks and may lead to death. However, the youngsters who had encountered the death of a close relative at a young age were less likely to 'play' with life through their teenage years. This suggests that the sooner children learn about death in a natural way, as part of life, the better.

Terminally ill children and adolescents

Interesting material is produced by the University of Rochester Online Medical Encyclopedia on the concept of death in terminally ill children. It indicates that that for a terminally ill child, past experience of death of a family member or pet, as well as age and emotional development, are what most influence a child's own concept of death. Interestingly, the article also notes that an adult's misconception and fears of death are often transferred to his children. A terminally ill infant has no real concept of death but will react to separation from known care-givers, painful procedures and an alteration in routine. Similarly, for a toddler the concept of death has little meaning, but he may pick up the emotions of the adults, of sadness, depression or anger, and then become upset or fearful.

The preschool child may begin to understand that death is feared by adults. The child may ask questions such as: why? and how? about their own condition, and feel guilt and shame that he has caused the adults' sadness. School-age children are developing a more realistic understanding, that death is permanent, universal and inevitable. Death may be personified as an angel, skeleton or ghost but the child fears because of uncertainty of what happens at death. Death is unknown, control is feared. There is separation from family and friends. The result for the terminally ill child is anxiety. An adolescent is beginning to establish his identity, independence from family and significance of the peer group. Adolescents may want their religious or cultural rituals observed. A characteristic of adolescence is feelings of immortality or being exempt from death. A terminally ill adolescent feels threatened facing death and changes in appearance brought about by treatment often result in feelings of aloneness or anger. It is important for parents and care-givers to realise that each child or adolescent is unique and needs a listener.

Believers' experiences – world faiths

Traditionally, for centuries religions have given meaning to life and death and hope of a life beyond death, but this has changed with the decline in the adherence to institutional Christianity and the increasing interest in spiritualities outside established and organised religion. The statistics of the 2011 Census of the population of England and Wales showed that within a population of 56.1 million, Christianity was the largest religious group at 33.2 million, a decline of more than four million since the census of 2001, contrasting with a rise of 1.2 million in Islam. Around one in four stated that they had no faith. The British Humanist Association said that the statistics on Christianity showed a significant cultural shift in a society where 'religious practice, identity, belonging and belief are all in decline...and non-religious identities are on the rise' (Battersby 2012). The UK is multicultural and its values diverse. It is also considered secular; that is, religious thinking, practice and institutions have lost their social significance.

In 2013, an independent Commission on Religion and Belief in British Public Life, convened by the Woolf Institute in Cambridge with the Rt. Hon. Baroness Elizabeth Butler-Sloss as its chair, was set up. It had 20 commissioners representing the major world faiths, academics, industrialists and politicians from across Great Britain and Northern Ireland and during its two-year project had local public hearings in Belfast, Birmingham, Cardiff, Glasgow, Leeds, Leicester and London. The final report was published on 7 December 2015 (Commission on Religion and Belief in British Public Life 2015). The Commission's purpose was 'to consider the place of religion and belief in contemporary Britain; to consider emerging trends and identities and to make recommendations for public life and policy'. The report noted dramatic changes in Britain's landscape in terms of religion and belief in the last half a century (p.9):

- The first is the increase in the number of people with non-religious beliefs and identities. Almost a half of the population today describes itself as non-religious, as compared with an eighth in England and a third in Scotland in 2001.

- The second is the general decline in Christian affiliation, belief and practice. Thirty years ago, two-thirds of the population would have identified as Christians. Today, that figure is four in ten, and at the same time there has been a shift away from mainstream denominations and a growth in evangelical and Pentecostal churches.

- The third is the increased diversity amongst people who have a religious faith. Fifty years ago Judaism – at one in 150 – was the largest non-Christian tradition in the UK. Now it is the fourth largest behind Islam, Hinduism and Sikhism. Although still comprising less than one in ten of the population, faith traditions other than Christian have younger age profiles and are therefore growing faster.

The report suggests that 'intra- and inter-faith disputes' linked with today's geopolitical crises across the Middle East and in parts of Africa and Asia reflect back on UK society creating or furthering tensions between communities. Ethno-religious issues and identities in the UK and globally are reshaping society in inconceivable ways and 'how we respond to such changes will have a profound impact on public life' (p.6).

In Section 6, 'Dialogue', the report recognises constructive dialogue between 'people holding different beliefs and worldviews, and belonging to different traditions and backgrounds' having 'vital roles to play in the tasks of building and maintaining relationships of mutual understandings and trust, and of strengthening the bonds of community' (p.49). The London Society of Jews and Christians was founded in 1927; the World Congress of Faiths in 1936 and the Council of Christians and Jews in 1942. 'Formal interreligious dialogue may be bilateral, trilateral or multilateral. Multilateral engagement is important in a shared society but is valuably supplemented by dialogue between two or three traditions, this can make it possible to go more deeply into painful shared histories which affect contemporary perceptions and experiences' (p.50). The report relates that the number of local interfaith organisations increased from 30 to over 230 between 1987 and 2015. For historic and numerical reasons these are between the Abrahamic faiths: 'there is scope for more bilateral dialogue between Abrahamic and Dharmic traditions' (p.52).

Section 4, 'Education', has significant reflections on Faith Schools – organisation, adherence policy, Collective Worship and Religious Education. It made recommendations concerning these topics. These will be returned to in Chapter 5, 'Schools Coping with Bereavement and Death', in the section on world faiths.

The twenty-first century began with incidents of global terrorism arising from deeply distorted religious ideologies and political, often racial, differences with bombings in New York in 2001 and London in 2005. At the beginning of the chapter reactions of adolescents to the atrocities were discussed. This century has heard voices expressing concerns on climate change becoming more strident with the fifth *Intergovernmental Panel on Climate Change – The Physical Science Basis* (27 October 2013), stating the threat to the existence of the cosmos. The sixth panel was in Paris in 2015. There was the fear of nuclear proliferation. Another concern was the world's sustainability for fresh water and food with a rise in world population projected from six and a half billion to nine billion by 2050. The global community has, through increased communications, become aware of the injustices and inequalities of the planet. The economic crisis of the developed countries resulted in the UK privatising sections of the NHS and freezing wages for many, leaving a socially divided, aimless and fragmented society. Yet institutional religion continued to be in the spotlight, its leaders making statements about political policy and its economic effects particularly on the poorest, raising media comments such as 'keep religion out of politics'.

Faith questions were raised in response to the loss of 3000 lives in the destruction of the World Trade Center (11 September 2001). In response, in the US, Sam Harris – author, neuroscientist and philosopher – blamed Islam, while directly criticising Christianity and Judaism. In the UK, it was Richard Dawkins's book *The God Delusion* (2006) that had impact. These writers are the new atheists: reductive materialists, who frequently criticise religion without understanding it, quoting biblical texts without contexts and confusing folk religion with reflective theology. In the context of the twenty-first century, a medicalised approach to death dominates; there is less conventional religious certainty, which results in doubts relating to a life after death, while there is a growth in spirituality.

Stephen Cave comments that death:

> is the point at which the profane and sacred collide – an event completely natural and yet surrounded by mystery; steeped in the physical realities of bodily processes, yet enwreathed with existential hopes and fears…many in the secular west and beyond, who have

been unmoored from the spiritual certainties of the past, seem to have concluded that it is best not to think about it at all. (2015, p.6)

The major belief systems of the world have wrestled with the mystery of death. We live in a multicultural society. Many children and adolescents attend schools in urban and suburban areas with a diversity of ethnic groups. Each group will have distinct rites and practices associated with death, some religious, others not. A useful resource for understanding death and bereavement across cultures is Parkes, Laungani and Young (1997).

The Abrahamic faiths of Judaism, Christianity and Islam have a common origin, but within each faith there are different expressions, for example Conservative and Liberal, Protestant and Catholic, Shia and Sunni Muslims. The Eastern faiths of Hinduism, Buddhism and Sikhism emerged from very different cultures, some of which have been moderated by Western culture, though each believes in an afterlife.

Judaism

In Judaism, life is valued above all else. Death is not a tragedy, even when it occurs early in life; it is a natural process. Our deaths, like our lives, have meaning and are all part of God's plan. The book of Genesis reflects life through stories, rather than abstract ideas. Jews believe that humans are created in the 'image' and 'likeness' of God (Genesis 1.27). Hebrew faith is down to earth. The Jews did not begin by worshipping the one God, the Creator. God in the Exodus delivered them from slavery and brought them into existence from nothing, establishing a Covenant relationship. This led them to believe that this must be the God who created the world. Genesis 1–11 is an ancient and composite text dealing with the universal themes of our human experience: good and evil; setting out why we need to be saved, from what and for what; and why God is doing it the way God is. There are four different pictures of creation (Genesis 1.1–2.4; 2.4b–3.24; Psalms 74.12–17 and 89.5–18; Proverbs 8.22–31), each emerging from a different experience and raising questions about life, faith and the world. Humanity is a paradox, created in the image and likeness of God (Genesis 1.26), 'a little lower than God' (Psalms 8.5–8), 'given dominion over the works of God's hands' (Genesis 1.26), yet people are self-centred, living in broken relationships with others and with God (Genesis 3).

The stories of the Creation, scholars believe, are influenced by other stories in the Ancient Near East (ANE) and brought back from the Jewish exile in Babylon. Genesis 1.1–2.4 is a poem in which order is created from chaos, separating light from dark, ending with the creation of humans and the Sabbath. The climax is not humanity but the Sabbath, a day for God's blessing and worship of the Creator. It is possibly a hymn explaining the significance of the Sabbath. Underlying the story are theological insights. God is a loving Creator and Sustainer. There is delight in the material world. The personification of 'Wisdom', present at creation, 'rejoices in the world and delights in the human race' (Proverbs 8.27–31 and Psalms 104). Christian history has often not taken the material world seriously, seeing it as either infected by sin or despising it because it is inferior to the spiritual, but our bodies are 'material'; the alienation of body dividing it from spirit is not Hebraic but the influence of Greek philosophy. The story witnesses to the interdependence of life, plant and animal. 'Then God said, "Let us make humankind in our image according to our likeness"' (Genesis 1.26): humans are unique in their relationship with the Creator. In the ANE, kings were held to be in 'the image of God', that is they were God's representatives. In Genesis, humans represent God in caring for creation (1.26), but what of likeness? Origen (184–253) distinguished between 'man', 'receiving the honour of God's image in his first creation, whereas the perfection of God's likeness was reserved for him at the consummation' (the end of time). Irenaeus explained this as Adam and Eve being like innocent children who needed to grow in self-consciousness to become morally aware adults.

The second Creation story (Genesis 2.4b–3.24) is from a human perspective, here the 'Lord God formed man from the dust of the ground, and breathed into his nostrils the breath of life and the man became a living being' (Genesis 2.7). The Hebrew word *ruach* means 'breath' and is physical and spiritual. Spirit is embodied in the world; if God withdraws *ruach* everything disintegrates into dust (Psalms 104.29) The breath of God's life, 'fills the world and holds together all things' (Wisdom 1.7). When the breath of a man leaves him, he expires and dies. The Hebrew word *nephesh* is translated as 'life/soul/ spirit/self/flesh'. Humanity is both physical and spiritual, holistic. We use the expression 'embodied'. The idea is reinforced by a wordplay on the name Adam (human/earthling) and the Hebrew word *adamah* meaning earth. Central to the Creation stories is the uniqueness of humans as created to reflect and be in communion with their Creator: humans may be, as the cosmologists today tell us, 'the debris of exploding stars', but within us is 'the breath of God'.

Genesis 3 is a story illustrating the difference between the goodness of God's creation and humanity's disobedience and death. It begins in a garden paradise of harmony between man and woman, humanity and God. There is one condition: God commands the humans not to eat the fruit of a particular tree. A serpent questions Eve, casting doubt about God's intentions. Eve saw the fruit, ate and gave it to her husband. They became aware of their nakedness and were ashamed, covering their genitals and hiding from God. Questioned by God, they blamed each other, then the serpent. They were punished – expelled from the garden – since humanity had become like God, for in knowing good and evil, they might, 'Take from the Tree of Life and live for ever'. The story suggests the entry of death into the world as punishment for the sin of disobedience; immortality is lost and humans become mortal. This is also suggested in the Wisdom Literature (538 BCE), 'for God created us for in-corruption and made us in the image of his own eternity but through the devil's envy death entered into the world' (Wisdom 2.23–24). The serpent becomes the devil. This is an anachronism of later Persian influence since in the ANE the snake was often associated with wisdom and the human potential for discernment. In the Rabbinic tradition, the Torah is identified with Wisdom and is the Tree of Life through which God, 'Planted eternal life within us' (Proverbs 3.13–18; 11.30; 13.12; 15.4).

Judaism considers Genesis 1–3 as a parable of the human condition, not history. Adam's responsibility for the sins of humanity, the entry of death into the world and the doctrine of inherited sin is not found in mainstream Judaism, which teaches that humans are born sin-free and later choose to sin and bring suffering on themselves. Inherited sin is considered a Greek, Pauline Christian interpretation and not a Hebrew concept (Barr 1992; Berger and Wyschogrod 1996; Magonet 2004). For Jews, Genesis 1–3 is life-affirming; though aware of sin, blessing dictates the agenda.

Gradually, in Judaism there developed hints of a shadowy life after death joining the departed in the underworld; 'Sheol' is Hebrew for 'the land of forgetfulness', or Hades in the Greek of the Septuagint (LXX). There are 65 biblical references to the descent to Sheol. For

Jews, the idea of existence after death without a body was unthinkable; a human is embodied. Centuries later the concept of resurrection developed. Resurrection would involve a body, in a world created and renewed. It is likely that this belief was due to Jewish apocalyptic thinking, arising from the experience of the Maccabean Revolt (168/7–164 BCE) against the Greek overlord Antiochus Epiphanes. Justice was demanded. God was just and must reward the faithful violated martyrs of the Maccabean family. This crisis of faith led to the answer of a double, this-worldly, resurrection: to life for those loyal to God under persecution and condemnation for the disloyal (Daniel 12.1–4). Scholars suggest reasons for the rise of thinking of a soul: the influence of Zoroastrianism, the religion of the Medes and Persians conquerors of the Jews (539–333 BCE); or the Greek conquest and Greek philosophy experienced by Jews of the Dispersion (333–160 BCE, cf. Wisdom 3 and 5 and 4 Maccabees). From the second century BCE, the rise of mystery religions such as the Mithraism faith of the Roman soldiers, known to have been brought to the UK from remains of a temple found in the City of London, helped ideas of a soul and its afterlife to develop further.

During the years that followed, there was hope for a better life for God's people. Yet God's promises for life, blessing and hope seemed to end in failure. Disillusioned, the writers concluded that if their belief was not fulfilled by human activity, it would be in a final Judgement led by a Messiah. Apocalyptic literature expressed the hope that God would defeat the powers of sin and death and establish a kingdom in this world. It is likely that this thinking emerged in the first century CE, when Jews were persecuted. For some, God's righting of injustice would be in a new world, a Garden of Eden. The central belief was that, 'at the end of history, God will resurrect the dead and restore them to full bodily existence' (Levenson 2006, p.ix). In the Gospels, there is a clear difference between Jewish groups: the Sadducees who did not accept resurrection and the Pharisees who did. Some Jews found a belief in God's goodness no longer possible; the only immortality was living on in the mind of God.

In Judaism, there is little development of a theology of an afterlife since it is unknown; what Jews know is the present, which they live to the full, in just lives, worshipping and honouring God.

Christianity

Christianity is rooted in Judaism and inherited the Hebrew Scriptures. It has a great deal to say about eternal life: a gift of God, evidenced in a quality of life not interrupted by death (John 3.16, 36; 4.14). The defeat of death was affirmed by the resurrection of Jesus, though his body is described as different from the one before the crucifixion. We are embodied and need a body to be human, yet we know that at death our physical body disintegrates. Paul (in 1 Corinthians 15.50–3) wrestles with this thinking: 'Flesh and blood cannot inherit the kingdom of God nor the perishable inherit the imperishable. Listen I will tell you a mystery. We will not all die but we will all be changed.' Paul uses the metaphor of the seed sown which must die to be transformed into new life (1 Corinthians 15.35–8). There is also teaching by Jesus of judgement during life and at death based not on belief but on actions of care for the sick, homeless and dispossessed (Matthew 25).

Paul, in his letter to the Romans 5.12f., has some of Christianity's most challenging, controversial and distinctive doctrine that sin 'came into the world through one man, and death came through sin…all have sinned'. Paul suggests that Adam's sin and guilt were inherited by later generations, but 'so one man's act of righteousness leads to justification and life for all', Christ as a second Adam, righting Adam's sin and death and bringing eternal life (Romans 5.21). However, the idea of inherited sin is not present in Genesis 3 and is denied by the Hebrew prophets (Jeremiah 31.29–31 and Ezekiel 18.2–4).

The doctrine of Original Sin was developed by Augustine (354–430 CE), influential in the Western Church's theology and interpretation of Genesis 3. He taught that Adam and Eve's act of disobedience led to feelings of shame evidenced in an uncontrollable stirring of the genitals, so that they covered themselves. He used the word concupiscence (desire) for the act of procreation through which sin, he believed, was transferred to successive generations. The Greek fathers such as Irenaeus and the Orthodox Church emphasise the cosmic dimension of the Fall; because of Adam, humans are born into a fallen world, but though fallen, are not deprived of free will. It is not a 'fall' but a failure to develop into the fullness of being human. Today, the Roman Catholic Church teaches that humans are made in the image of God, and within are urges of good and evil. Because of the effects of Original Sin humans inherit a fallen nature. Humans do not bear 'original guilt' from Adam and Eve's disobedience, though 'the devil' has acquired a certain hold on humans. Anglicanism follows Luther in teaching that humans inherit Adam's guilt and are in a state of sin from their conception. This is reflected in the baptism of children to cleanse them from the 'Original Sin' inherited through birth. Douglas Davies notes that Christianity may be defined as both positive and negative in attitudes to death. The positive is that death, the outcome of sin, is overcome through the love of Christ, the comfort of the Spirit and God's ultimate faithfulness; this is Good News. Negative is that death is 'the central moral pivot around which God works with the cross as its symbol' (Davies 2008, p.8). It is death conquered by life, but 'there remains a certain Christian romantic commitment to death as evil that can be adjudged as less than valuable' (Davies 2008, pp.8–9). Western Christianity has tended to emphasise guilt and sin, which is prominent in the Roman Catholic theology of the Mass. In the Protestant theology the emphasis is on Christ's Cross and in a literalist interpretation of Genesis 3. In the Eastern Orthodox tradition there is an emphasis on God's glory and love. This emphasis can be seen dramatically in the difference in interior architecture between Orthodox and Catholic churches.

Islam

Islam has roots in both Judaism and Christianity; for Mohammed, this world was transitory, though Muslims give credence to it because it is what they experience. The true life is after death, and this belief is an act of faith: the Qur'an states, 'Who will give life to bones while they are disintegrating?... He will give them life who produced them the first time; and He is, of all creation, Knowing' (Qur'an 36.78–80). The Muslim is accountable for the way he lives, because behaviour shapes future character. Life after death is necessary – a response to God's attributes. God's justice and mercy have no meaning if there is no life after death. It is characterised by a day of judgement, the fires of hell or the garden paradise of heaven. In Islam, the word Jahannam derives from Gehenna; the Qur'an contains 77 references to it.

Hinduism and Buddhism

Within these faiths, this life is the first of many lives. The way of life now, particularly the believer's concern for the marginalised, affects life beyond this one. This belief is expressed in the law of Karma, the essence of which is that our past determines who we are and will be. This doctrine is a reincarnation of a life until the final goal of being one with the ultimate, the Supreme Being, is reached – *moksha* – or entering the deathless state of Nirvana. The Hope of Nirvana is the fusion of the soul with the body but the body is of no importance – it is the soul that matters.

For Hindus, all created life is sacred. The law of Karma has a more subtle and complex character. John Hick comments that it is not the present conscious self that is reborn. Rather, 'In each incarnation there is a new empirical self, which comes into existence at conception and ceases at death' (Hick 1983, p.491). Underlying the series of selves is an eternal spiritual reality, the *jiva*. This is manifest in various expressions, including the physical body, which perishes at death and the 'subtle body', *linga sharira*, which lives beyond death and 'is later re-embodied by attaching itself to a developing embryo' (p.491). The subtle body bears the individual Karma, and selects the appropriate kind of birth. Memories of previous lives exist only in the *jiva*. In the last earthly life, the individual has transcended self-centredness, and is 'consciously one with the universal atman, or self, which is ultimately identical with Brahman, the eternal absolute Reality' (p.491).

Buddhism believes in the brotherhood of all creation. Sickness and death are accepted as natural to life with a continuous cycle of birth and rebirth through the diverse forms of animal life until perfected. It is similar to Hinduism, 'except that which is successively reborn is not a continuing entity, the Karma-bearing "subtle body", but the stream of karma itself' (Hick 1989, p.491). The Advaita Hindu and the Theravada Buddhist practise meditation and mindfulness and consciously avoid the domination of human desires and passions in their spiritual quest of identification with the divine.

Drawing together experience and cultural context leading to practical implications

As adults, we try to protect our children and shield them from harm. However, if we try to protect them from the reality of death, or try to manipulate the reality of death for them by ignoring their questions, refusing to let them talk of the deceased or using euphemisms of the dead, we are likely to cause them more harm and distress in the long run. Depression in adults is often associated with unresolved grief.

Young children have a healthier approach to death and dying than adults. The very young have enquiring minds and ask many questions. They are fascinated by death in animals, for instance that of wild birds and pets. It is not morbid to allow children to talk about death since it is part of their inquisitive nature and desire to make sense of the world and their own experience of it. This fascination is noted in the quotation at the heading of each chapter. It may seem macabre, for example, but Diane loves going to clean her grandfather's grave with her grandmother. Diane is ten years old. In contrast, there is still a taboo in the adult world about talking of death, though in recent years this has been challenged. Death becomes the butt of jokes: Woody Allen said, 'It's not that I'm afraid of dying. I just don't want to be there when it happens.' In contrast, the German theologian Jürgen Moltmann stated that 'to live as if there were no death is to live an illusion. Death acts as a catalyst to plunge us into more authentic life modes and it enhances our pleasure in the living of life' (Moltmann 1996, p.50). An excellent illustration of Moltmann's words is the life of Etty Hillesum, a Dutch Jewish woman who died in Auschwitz in 1943. It is described in a book by Patrick Woodhouse (2009).

Michael Morpurgo, at one time Children's Literature Laureate of the UK, wrote, 'My role in life: to teach them (his grandchildren) about death' (Morpurgo 2006, p.5). This role emerged from an experience in his childhood. The news of his grandfather's death was given to him at boarding school. It was not grieved so left Morpurgo with many questions and with fears of death. Years later, his grandmother died. On this occasion, he saw his grandmother's body and came to an understanding of death as simply an end. 'We need intimations of mortality – for my grandchildren it may well be the last useful thing I can do for them' (p.5).

As adults, we need to engage with our own deaths in order that we can be alongside, help and learn from children. Children's concepts of death, as all their concepts, develop in stages. We need to recognise these stages and respond in appropriate ways.

The world faiths have responded to questions of death and its origins through stories called myths: a literary device to explore a deep insight in a concrete, pictorial way, to explore truth concerning the significance of death. These stories are universal and are ones that children can explore. I return to the use of literature with children in helping them understand death in Chapter 5. Death is a reality but more importantly a catalyst in order that we might recognise its finality and enjoy our living.

ACTIVITIES TO ELICIT THE READER'S EXPERIENCE

Thoughts on Death and Dying

Answer these questions quietly and on your own. Notice your emotions as you do it – jot them down.

1. When as a child, and how, did you first learn about death (e.g. pet/ grandad)?

2. What were your feelings?

3. What thoughts/feelings have you inherited from this childhood experience about death?

4. How often now do you think about your own death?

   Daily   Occasionally   Never

5. At what age would you like to die?

6. Is there anything you want to resolve/ ask forgiveness for/be thankful for before you die?

7. Where would you like to die? (Include the sounds/sights/smells around you.)

8. Who would you like to be with you?

9. What are they saying to you?

10. What would you want to say to them?

11. What concerns you most about dying?

12. Will faith help you when you die?

13. What does 'death' mean to you?

14. What do you believe about the afterlife? Where does this belief come from?

15. Have you ever talked about dying and death with any one? Give examples.

2

Grief and Bereavement

Heaven is not a place. It's just an idea. But it is a very strong idea, because if we didn't have it we wouldn't have any hope.

(Andy in Marshall 2003, p.25)

A child's experience

Alex was six. He had a guinea pig, which on the whole he remembered to feed, though his mother often had to remind him, and some days it got twice the amount of food it should have and some days none. One summer day, he went out into the garden to look at the guinea pig in its hutch. All was silent, and Alex could not understand it. He opened the door of the hutch and felt inside, calling the guinea pig. Nothing happened. He found the guinea pig and felt that it was cold and lifeless. It was dead. Taking it in his hands, he went sobbing to his mother. 'It's dead,' he said through his crying, 'but where has the guinea pig man gone to?'

Reflection on experience

Children need to be taken seriously. Alex's grief was real and tangible. His grief is commensurate with that of a six-year-old. The guinea pig was physically dead – but somehow that was not enough for Alex. There was something more which he simply called, 'the guinea pig man'. Where had 'the guinea pig man' gone? What was Alec questioning?

An adolescent's experience

Patricia was twelve; she had leukaemia and was in hospital. Patricia knew that she was dying. When the consultant, who was a Christian, tried to talk about death and a next life in order to prepare her, Patricia told her to 'piss off'. I was sent for as the chaplain by the consultant to sort out Patricia. I had met Patricia before, and I knew she loved and enjoyed jokes, so I went to see her armed with a Spike Milligan joke book. We chatted and joked. Eventually, I asked her if she had seen the consultant recently. She simply said that the consultant wanted to talk about death. 'But I didn't,' she said. 'I know that I won't be here much longer. I don't need her to tell me about heaven and all that claptrap. I want to live.' She stopped talking. 'What do you enjoy about living?' I asked. There was no reply. She had fallen asleep laughing at one of the jokes in my book.

Later that week I heard that Patricia had died. The family asked me to take her funeral. When I visited the home, a farmworker's cottage, Patricia's body was lying on the settee, the cat curled up on her feet and her brother and sister playing near her.

Reflection on experience

Patricia was a lively youngster who was facing death. Her consultant, with the best will in the world, spoke to her of her death. Perhaps as a professional her approach could have been more careful. I tried to meet Patricia where she was. What had she meant when she said that she wanted to live? Was it that she wanted to live every moment until her end whenever that was? Or that she wanted to conquer her disease? I don't know, but everything in the room where her body was laid at home seemed so natural; the atmosphere suggested that death was not to be feared but to be lived. Her siblings, though likely to be missing her, were getting on with life. Patricia was upfront, wanting quality of life while she had it. Adults tend to be more aware of the past – regrets for those things that were not done, opportunities missed – and the future, wondering what will happen. We forget to live in the present, the only place we can live.

Linking adult, child and adolescent experience

Grief following bereavement is normal for adults, children and adolescents but is not easy. In research done by ComRes almost half of Britons, 47 per cent, say they would feel uncomfortable talking to someone who has been recently bereaved. Significant numbers of bereaved people have experienced negative reactions to their grief, including others avoiding them, crossing the road, ceasing to invite them to dinner and even the total loss of a friendship (ComRes 2014). However, the UK sociologist Grace Davie suggested the beginning of a change of attitude to grief. Davie researched the response to the death of Diana, Princess of Wales, in a car crash in Paris in 1997. Following the news of Diana's death, flowers were laid by the public outside Kensington Gardens and Buckingham Palace as expressions of grief by those who had never met the princess. There was a great outpouring of grief. At St James's Palace a book of condolence was opened and others were opened across the country. Grace Davie commented that expressions of grief at Diana's death gave people permission to express the suppressed grief of their own bereavements (Davie 2000). More recently thousands visited the Tower of London between July and November 2014 to see an exhibition of ceramic poppies, which is now on tour in the UK. Each poppy represents a soldier killed in the past World Wars, but it also evokes in families memories of their own bereavements.

Emotions as a result of loss are normal, for bereavement is not an illness, nor is it pathological. Children in particular are frequently not considered as having feelings and understanding about death, yet they are great observers of their environment and the grieving of people around them; their emotions must not be underestimated. Young children in particular are fascinated by death. However, at a family death, the adults are so wrapped up in their own grief that they may forget or ignore children and even refuse to let children talk about the deceased or attend the funeral. At the death of her husband, grandma refused to talk about him. A grandson who loved his grandfather spent more and more time alone in his bedroom refusing to talk. His family, not understanding the reasons for his silence, were so worried that they made an appointment for him to see a child psychiatrist. Talking began the journey to facing the grandson's bereavement. Adults surrounding a child need not hide their own grief, since it may help a child to realise grief is normal, nor should a child be moved to a 'protected environment' away from a dying parent with a terminal illness. It is not unusual for a bereaved child to develop similar symptoms to that of the dying or dead person, mirroring the death. Children need to be respected and informed of what is happening in a situation of terminal illness and of death itself. It is the sensitivity shown to a child and adolescent and knowing how to respond to them that is significant.

Children and adolescents experience a range of emotions in bereavement; they grieve differently from adults since they are still developing their understanding and coping with life and therefore with death. For young children, when someone close to them dies it is a new experience, and they are unprepared for its impact. However, adults have usually experienced death. Winston's Wish, a major UK bereavement charity for children, suggests that while adult grief is constant and long lived, a child's grief can seem more like leaping in and out of puddles: one minute a child may be sobbing, the next minute asking what is for tea (Crossley 2000). This behaviour may seem callous to adults in the family, an 'acting up'. If adults see the child only during moments like this and not during the moments of intense sadness and loss, the adult may ignore the fact that children grieve. The American psychologist Esther Shapiro suggests that children oscillate, putting their grief down then taking it up again. The grief of an adult is more consistent and is often hidden, since grief is frequently taboo in UK culture. A bereaved adult is expected to return to work immediately after the funeral and behave as if nothing has happened in her life. But if adults in the family try to protect a child from their own feelings and grief by remaining silent about the person who has died, the silence can stall the process of collective grief in a family which helps positive grief to emerge.

Huw Spanner, writing on children and grief, refers to the changes in British society in the twenty-first century, which is characterised by fragmented communities, separated families and a decline in the practice of religion and other rituals which in the past were markers of the process of bereavement. Spanner suggests that:

> our culture has made childhood into something of a fetish. Children are supposed to be carefree and innocent, and so the proper thing seems to be to shield them from anything grim or unpleasant. Even though (perversely) they are exposed to unreal and inconsequential forms of death – in films and computer games. (Spanner 2007, p.22)

A result of this has been the reluctance in adults to talk about death to children. Children have been called 'the forgotten mourners' (Smith 1999). If a child is not included in the grief of the family, she may feel guilty for the death and think that she said or did something that caused the death. For example, guilt may follow if the child had a row with Dad before Dad went out and was involved in a fatal car accident. Guilt might also emerge when a child has forgotten the death in the family and is having fun, and suddenly realises what she is doing. On these occasions, the child could be reminded that a deceased parent would want her to enjoy life.

A child will need to revisit a parental loss since as she gets older she will miss the deceased in new ways and will need to know more of the truth of the reasons for the death. For instance, an occasion of revisiting might be when adolescence is reached and a girl misses her mum being able to help her with a 'prom' graduation outfit. Spanner states that the consequence of neglect of grief in a child can be substantial long-term damage, 'feelings of guilt, inadequacy, isolation and confusion can erode a child's natural resilience…lead to underachievement at school and in the worst cases, exclusion, anti-social behaviour…mental illness and the inability to maintain relationships' (Spanner 2007, p.22). Understanding the unique grief of children and responding well to it are essential. Grieving is a natural process: children, as adults, need to know that there is no right way to grieve. It can include anger, sobbing and silence. Grief varies across cultures.

Sociological, psychological and historical insights into grief

Bereavement is the most psychologically distressing experience that most people encounter. It is useful to have some definitions. Grieving and mourning are not the same. Alan Billings defines grieving as, 'our personal, emotional response to the death of our loved ones' (Billings 2002, p.74). This may be expressed as:

emotions such as anger, guilt, fear, relief, sadness;

thoughts – processes like understanding, and believing that the person is gone;

physical responses such as sleeplessness, stomach-aches, headaches or loss of appetite;

spiritual questioning about the meaning and significance of life and for some the existence and nature of God.

(The Dougy Center 2008, p.5)

Mourning is 'the behaviour which particular social groups deem appropriate in the face of death' (Billings 2002, p.74). It is public and intentional such as talking and crying, or often with adolescents, risk-taking behaviour. All children and adolescents who experience a death grieve, though they may not mourn. The distinction is critical: it must not be assumed that an individual is not grieving because there is no public reaction. It is assumed that grieving is natural, universal and purely psychological, but mourning is determined by culture. Billings maintains that both are influenced by culture (Billings 2002, p.74). The UK sociologist Tony Walter adds a definition of bereavement as 'the objective state of having lost someone or something' (Walter 1999, p.xv). He argues that 'culture affects grief as well as mourning, and indeed grief underlies the very constitution of society' (p.xv).

Models of grieving
Worden's model
A well-known model is that of Worden who proposed the thinking that grief is a process and not a fixed 'state'. People need to work through their reactions in order to make a complete adjustment. He drew on Freud's concept of grief work, Bowlby's attachment theory, developmental psychology and Engel's concept of grief as an illness. Worden recognised that humans have, and are, narratives or stories in that we are 'made up' of all the people, events and places we have experienced in our lives. However, change and re-creation are necessary for each of us as we build on previous memories and incorporate new

experiences such as the death of someone close. Change requires re-definition of ourselves and our 'world' in an ongoing 'creation story'. Grief and loss in bereavement are significant parts of our life story and common to all humans. Worden understood grief as a process of re-visioning the world, ourselves and our place within the world. He thought of grief as having four overlapping tasks:

- to accept the reality of the loss

- to experience the pain of grief

- to adjust to an environment in which the deceased is missing

- to let go, that is, to withdraw emotional energy from the relationship with the deceased and to redirect the energy. The deceased is not forgotten but rather the influence of the person on my life is integrated into memory and my life story.

(adapted from Worden 1996, p.45)

The Whirlpool

Richard Wilson, a consultant paediatrician, has suggested a model of grief called 'The Whirlpool'. He uses an image of life as a river running smoothly until it falls over a cliff edge; this is a picture of a 'waterfall of loss':

> The waterfall of bereavement when the river turns into individual droplets of water thrown out in all directions, is a state of shock, numbness, and denial…then the chaotic water hits the pool below and forms a whirlpool of grief – a state of falling apart, of emotional chaos. The water can hit the rocks around the pool, producing pain and physical symptoms in the griever. Or it can wash up on the opposite bank and stay stuck there. But eventually, the water from the whirlpool flows on through mourning to an acceptance that loss is real, but life can carry on. (Ward 1993, pp.65–66)

A helpful diagram of this can be found in image 43 ('Bereavement, Loss and Grief, Survival Strategy for Primary Care') in Ward *et al.* (1995).

The Chaplain of Magdalen College School, Oxford, working with a teenager whose best friend had died, heard how the youngster's grief came in huge waves. The Chaplain used the image of 'waves' to suggest that the teenager thought of surfing in Cornwall. Two things could happen with huge waves: either you tumble them and go with the flow or ride them. Practice enables you to ride more of them (Lawton 2014, p.12).

The Grief Wheel

This is a model used by Social Services in the UK, having recognised and needing to work with the link between juvenile delinquency and unattended and unresolved loss in their adolescent clients (Grief Education Institute 1986). The incidence of memories of childhood bereavement not dealt with in youth offenders can be up to 40 per cent, ten times higher than the national average of 4 per cent. These losses were not just about death, though many were, but included the loss through parental divorce, illness, and injury (YoungMinds 2013). The Grief Wheel indicates the need for moving through four phases, each phase merging into the next, but with some movement backwards and forwards. No time scale is given for the grieving process. The phases are as follows:

Shock: This is when the reality of the loss has simply not sunk in. Emotions include numbness of feeling; disbelief; euphoria; unemotional and suicidal thoughts of wanting to be with the deceased.

Protest: This occurs when the bereaved protests that the loss cannot be real, while confronted with evidence that it is real. Emotions include sadness; guilt – 'if only'– and fear of his or her own death; preoccupation with memories; searching for the deceased; physical distress such as sleep disturbance.

Disorganisation: This happens when the reality of the loss is only too real. Examples of reaction are confusion, apathy, loss of interest; anxiety and the loss of any sense of meaning in life.

Reorganisation: This occurs when the bereaved begins to rebuild his or her life. This is a time of developing balanced and more realistic memories of the deceased; pleasure in remembering; a return to previous levels of functioning and new insight and purpose in life.

(Grief Education Institute 1986)

The Grieving Wheel

This model was developed and is used by a hospice in Yukon USA (Hospice Yukon n.d.). The model recognises that each loss is unique and yet there is a commonality in grief. The Grieving Wheel helps us reflect upon these normal responses to loss as recurring cycles in our lives. Beginning at the top with 'Life as usual', we move around the wheel, often swinging back and forth between the four phases. The four phases are shown as a circle: Life as usual; Shock; Chaos and New beginnings, returning to the beginning. Then a major loss occurs and a new journey begins. The first reaction is a state of 'Shock', perhaps being unable to believe or comprehend what has happened. We long to return to life as usual, but eventually we come to acknowledge our loss. The second reaction, moving round the Wheel, is one of resistance. Reactions are intense pain, anger, sadness, guilt, despair, loneliness, depression and hopelessness. Emotions feel overwhelming like 'Chaos'. This stage is a very significant one in the journey through grief. Understanding the grieving process can help us realise that suffering will end and lead towards our healing, and with this we can find the courage to stay present to the 'Chaos'. As we adjust, we come to a new way of thinking about life, a new understanding. The process turns to 'New beginnings' as we are able to begin the process of 'Integration'. The Wheel is complete and we are back where we started with 'Life as usual', yet we are different people because of the experience of bereavement, for this is not a simple circle but a spiral of growth.

The American psychologist J.A. Graham believes that grieving after a loss consists of psychological tasks that children work through progressively:

1. The first phase involves 'understanding what death is, knowing its characteristics, and being able to recognize when it has happened'. For the child it is important to feel 'self-protected', that is they know someone has died but that neither the child nor the family are in danger.

2. The middle phase involves 'understanding that death is a reality and accepting the emotions that come along with that realization'. This may include reflecting and having memories about the deceased, not that they will come back, but that the memories remain. There will be grief, but that of children

and adults is different, since the former have little experience of death, the latter do. It is children who have to spend time working out what has happened to the loved parent or godparent.

3. The last phase of the process involves 'a reorganisation of a child's sense of identity and his relationship with others and with the environment', in that since a child invests emotionally in relationships following a change in his surroundings through the absence of a person he is able not to fear death yet remember the deceased and carry the memories and any sadness with him.

(Graham 2013, p.2)

In some models, the emphasis was on moving through stages of bereavement to an 'acceptance' of the death, a letting go of the deceased. In the 1980s, there was a growing suspicion of professionals and those who said that emotional ties between the bereaved and their loved ones should be broken. Walter (1999, pp.19–20) suggested an integration, the bereaved carrying with them the deceased, since the latter was part of their present life story.

There is an upward spiral of grief which allows acceptance and then the return to an earlier stage; for example, if six months after a loss the bereaved feels really tearful and sad one day, she may worry that something is wrong. However, the person is likely to be in a different place to the black hole in the beginning; feelings may be the same but with less intensity. The bereaved will have moved on and made some adjustments. By using the spiral a bereaved person can alleviate the pressure of having to move on through the stages. It may become less frightening. The idea of acceptance can be misleading; it is rather 'adjustment' – the deceased is part of the bereaved's being and history.

Children's and adolescents' experiences of the grieving process

All children develop at different rates and it is important to remember that the parents know their own child the best. Winston's Wish states, 'A death in the family is always hard. It's even harder when you don't understand what death is' (Winston's Wish 2002, p.1). Chapter 1 indicated children's understanding of the concept of death in relation to ages. This knowledge forms the basis of how children grieve. We now look at the behaviour that emerges as a result of death and how adults can respond to a child's grief in a positive way to forward the child's grieving process.

Babies

A baby has not yet got any understanding of death. However, if the deceased is close to the baby, for example a parent who feeds or baths the child, there may well be 'separation anxiety'. Elizabeth Kübler-Ross notes that up to the age of three a child is concerned only about separation. This may be avoided if a familiar adult or parent is able to provide continuity and some normality. The baby may react by signs of irritability, some change in eating patterns which may become erratic, disturbance of sleeping patterns, crying or tummy upsets and temporary withdrawal from carers until security and stability are re-established. Providing support means keeping normal routines and structures whenever possible. Positive bereavement depends on nonverbal communications: physical care, affection, reassurances and the tone of voice. This is done by giving verbal and physical affection with words of reassurance which show healthy coping mechanisms. It is important to provide a warm, loving caretaker when the parent is not available.

Toddlers

Toddlers have no real understanding of death; however, they understand more than you might think. They can sense when there is excitement, sadness or anxiety in the home, when a significant person is missing or the presence of new people. A toddler will overhear conversations in a hushed voice. Her reactions are sensory and physical. Any child old enough to smile or express an emotive reaction to a situation is old enough to grieve. When verbal skills are limited, grief is expressed through behaviours and play.

The toddler is likely to become attached to another adult in the family. Behaviour may include crying; health problems such as skin rash, tummy upsets, coughs and colds; clinging, tantrums, erratic sleep patterns, fussy eating; repeated questions (within speech and language limitations) and the need for the adult to provide a repeated response and explanations. The responses given will vary with the needs and personality of the child and include consistent physical care, cuddles and comfort and maintaining a consistent routine. Responses can include activities such as messy paints, drawing, toys and puppets to encourage spontaneous, imaginative and creative play to help a child to express their feelings. Three-year-old Susie's mother had died at home. After this event Susie constantly wanted the book *Where the Wild Things Are* (Sendak 2000) read to her. In the story, Max in his wolf suit causes mischief. His mother sends him to his bedroom. Here everything changes, and he is taken to a faraway land of wild creatures who he faces by looking at them without blinking. The creatures submit to Max. When he returns home, his supper is waiting and 'it was still hot'. The story addresses facing and conquering the wild things in life. Could death be like this for a three-year-old, a horror you must face? The death of a parent is a threat to a child's whole life and the resources of the remaining parent may be limited. In this particular case, the father quickly went back to work, and a friend was able to move in to look after Susie and her older siblings for the first nine months of their bereavement. When Susie went out in her pushchair, she said to everyone she met whom she knew, 'My mummy's dead.' There are many books about loss for children, some of which are included in the Further Reading section at the end of the book. A comforter such as a blanket, dummy, pacifier or a particular soft toy may assume a special importance at this stage.

Three- to five-year-olds

Children of this age have a limited concept of death in which it is not final. Death is rather like going to sleep and waking up or going to work; believing the deceased will come back, young children may search for them. This may lead to an apparent lack of reaction when told about a death and the child may act inappropriately after news of a death, perhaps asking 'Can I have another biscuit now?' or to go out to play. Tantrums arising from insecurity and difficulty verbalising can result in acting out feelings in increased aggression – more irritable, aggressive play. The child often asks repeated questions in an attempt to make sense of the loss and these are often matter of fact; these may disturb and upset the adult, particularly if it is the death of a parent and the bereaved parent is trying to cope with her own grief. The experience of death undermines a child's confidence and her world becomes unreliable and insecure. She may cling to other adults in the family and not want to be parted from family members in case someone else 'disappears'. The child is only capable of showing sadness for short periods of time and then escapes into play or may exhibit little anxiety due to belief that the deceased is coming back.

Adult response needs to offer as much continuity as possible with routines and activities, which gives security in what may be a changing world for the child. A reassurance can be given, for example, 'I will pick you up after school'. Family can provide opportunities to play, draw and paint, helping the child to express feelings. Sharing books on death and loss which treat loss as something natural can help the child to verbalise feelings and fears and can also help to identify feelings and reactions. The child may need much physical affection.

Five- to nine-year-olds

A five- to -nine-year old begins to recognise that she too will die, which is a frightening concept and may lead to psycho-somatic symptoms such as headaches and chest and breathing pains. These may be the body's unconscious attempt to draw attention to mental distress. Behaviour may be aggressive – verbal and physical. Some children may play 'dead' in the playground. The child can see death as a 'taker' or 'spirit' that comes and gets you. Fear that death is contagious and other loved ones will 'catch it' and die too may result in a phobia about illness and doctors, a fear of the dark, nightmares and difficulty in getting to sleep, regression to an early stage of development such as baby talk, bedwetting, trying to gain attention or being afraid to go to school. This phobia is especially noticeable if a parent dies.

Children are sometimes fascinated by issues of mutilation and very curious about what the body looks like. They may connect death with violence and may ask, 'Who killed him?' yet may worry how the deceased can eat and breathe.

In response, it is important that the child is supported, reassured and listened to; it is important to be honest and tell a child if the adult has no answers. The adult should ask questions to ensure that the child's thinking is understood. It is important to avoid such clichés as: 'Don't worry, things will be OK', 'You're such a strong boy', and using euphemisms. Avoid, 'Grandma went to sleep and is now in heaven.' Instead say, 'Grandma was very sick and the sickness made her die.' It is important to identify specific fears, distortions and perceptions. For example, make sure the child does not feel responsibility and guilt and is not blaming herself for the death. Since language is still concrete, a child may have difficulty expressing feelings verbally. Patience is needed and answers to questions need to be concrete. Helping a child to share bad dreams is significant.

Children of this age need information and reassurance that life will go on for them, for example that they will be taken to football practice or dancing lessons, coupled with the reliability of other adults in keeping promises they have made. Having a pet can be significant, since touch is highly important, as is responsibility for the care of an animal, drawing or painting to express feelings and books which deal with loss and death. Adults should help a child with positive memories of the deceased and model healthy coping behaviours: give treats as well as routine; make a memory book; look at photos of the deceased; show physical affection; visit the cemetery together; do physical activities and read books together.

Nine- to eleven-year-olds

At the age of nine to eleven, the child's perception and understanding is nearer to that of adults. Children are aware of the finality of death and the impact the death has on them. With this comes a self-consciousness about fear of their own death, and if a parent has died, fear of a remaining parent dying. There is a concern with how their world will change; with the loss of the relationship often come blunt, factual questions: 'Who will go with me to football now?' These are sometimes called, 'landscape questions'; they are not self-centred, but the death of a parent is likely to mean change, for example the necessity of moving to a cheaper house or eventually a new 'step parent'. Change takes time. There is a fragile independence, a reluctance to open up delayed reactions. At first, it seems as if nothing has happened. Then grief reaction sets in, with increased anger and for some guilt over the death. There are mood swings and somatic symptoms.

At this age when friendships and groups are significant there may be disrupted relationships with peers and school phobia. There may be the beginning of developing an interest in rituals and the spiritual effects of life.

Providing support includes encouraging discussion of the child's concerns but be honest and tell her when you do not have an answer. Address the impulse towards acting out and allow a child the opportunity to identify their feelings. Allow for regressive behaviours. Avoid clichés such as, 'You must be strong, so I don't have to worry about you' or 'Big boys don't cry'. Gently relieve the child from attempts to take over adult responsibilities; this is particularly important when a girl has lost her mother and her father feels lost and becomes dependent on his daughter. Provide and encourage expressive experiences such as writing or drawing while modelling healthy coping behaviours.

Adolescence

Adolescence is an emotional time of upheaval with waves of differing feelings as a result of physical and hormonal changes. Finding a balance between dependence and independence is tough; the adolescent needs security yet boundaries to push against. Discovering and forming an identity is particularly hard if a parent dies when an adolescent is trying to achieve her own separation and identity yet relies on a parental gender and social role model. It is a time of rebellion and self-absorption, searching for meaning and a questioning of all that the family takes for granted. Since grief is predominantly emotional, adolescents are familiar with turbulent waters and often handle it better than adults do.

There is likely to be an increased capacity to see a situation from another person's perspective – for example, empathy with the parents of a peer group friend who has died, or empathy with their parent on the loss of one of their own parents – but this can fluctuate, with the adolescent having episodes of self-centred thinking. Adolescents have special needs. They oscillate between forgetting and remembering; the unremitting pace of adult grief is too intense, too much an interference with the necessary work of growing up. Certain books are helpful (see the sections for Key Stages 3 and 4 in the Further Reading section at the end of the book).

Believers' experiences – world faiths

Judaism

There is an immense diversity of practice within Judaism, since 25 per cent of Jews in the UK do not belong to a synagogue. There are secular Jews, Conservative, Orthodox, Reformed and Liberal Jews. The notes here represent the rituals of many Orthodox Jews.

In Judaism death is a natural process. The grief process is not an expression of fear or of distaste for death. It has two purposes: to show respect for the dead, *kayod ha-met*, and to comfort the living who will miss the deceased, *nihum avelim*. Grief is a marked time with prescribed, detailed and practical rituals, allowing the full expression of grief, while discouraging excesses of grief and letting the mourner gradually return to normality. This period must be a comfort to Jews, since decisions do not have to be made at a time when emotions may be raw as a way is mapped out beforehand, giving a framework for the psyche to begin processing the loss.

Within Judaism, mourning is at home: in the *Shiva* house, the house of mourning of the close relatives parents, spouses, children and siblings. A memorial candle is lit (*yahrzeit*), which symbolises the soul of the dead and in some homes mirrors are covered. When a person dies, adult or child, traditionally the family tear clothes; if the death is of a child the parent tears clothing over the heart. The blessing is recited which describes God as the 'true judge', an acceptance of God's taking of the life. A period of a day or two follows when the family are left alone to allow the full expression of grief. Burial takes place as soon as possible, after which a close relative or near neighbour prepares the first meal for the mourners, the meal of condolence. Traditionally this consists of eggs, a symbol of life, and bread. After this visitors are permitted. *Shiva*, the next period of mourning, begins on the day of burial and lasts seven days. Mourners sit on low stools or the floor instead of chairs, do not wear leather shoes and men stop shaving and cutting their hair. Women do not wear cosmetics, do not work and in traditional families abstain from actions for pleasure such as bathing, having sex, putting on fresh clothes or study, except for the *Torah*. These are markers of loss and of the utter separation of bereavement from daily life. Mourners wear the torn clothes they wore when recognising the death. Prayer services are held with friends. If the Sabbath occurs during *Shiva* it counts as one day. The next period of mourning is known as *Shloshim*, meaning 30, because it lasts until the thirtieth day after burial. During this period mourners do not attend parties or celebrations; men do not shave or cut their hair nor listen to music (de Lange 1987, pp.128–9). The final period of mourning is *avelut* and this lasts for a year after burial. The son of the deceased recites daily the *Kadesh*: 'May His great name grow exalted and sanctified in the world that he created as he willed. May he give reign to his Kingship in your lifetimes and in your days... Amen.' This is an affirmation of faith in God and might seem strange at the death of a child, yet it expresses a belief in a Being beyond, which Jews hold despite possible feelings of anger and injustice at such a young death.

Christianity

Suffering and death, particularly of the young, raises many questions for those who believe in a loving, all powerful God. Children and adolescents are quick to ask, 'Why did it happen?' when someone they know and love dies, particularly if it is a child they know. The response of Iris Murdoch in her novel *The Unicorn* (1966) was: 'Suffering is no scandal. It is natural... All creation suffers. It suffers from having been created, if from nothing else. It suffers from being divided from God.'

The children at an after school club were exploring the bible story of the rivalry between the brothers Esau and Jacob who were twins (Genesis 27.1–46). Tom, a seven-year-old, suddenly blurted out, 'I'm a twin.' No one knew this. Tom continued, 'She died 'cos I was stronger and pushed her out of the way as we were being born, so she died.' There was silence. Tom's underlying sense of guilt was palpable. In one moment, he had raised issues of responsibility, guilt, shame, death and loss. The adult leaders wondered how Tom knew about his birth and could only assume that it was still significant in the conversations and grieving of his parents. The occasion opened the 'flood gates' for other children to share their losses, one that needed pastoral care and sensitivity for Tom in particular but also for the other children in the group.

There are no answers to the question of suffering for most Christians, although there are those who see suffering as a punishment from God. I find this impossible to accept since suffering and death are no respecter of persons. There are exceptions such as terminal and inherited conditions and the suffering that is self-inflicted, such as that of a heavy smoker when the risks of cancer from this are known. The Christian belief is that God created the world, and death and disease are part of that world. Through the love of friends and family God's love can be experienced: a love that does not end in death, but is the beginning of something more. Grief is important, as noted in several biblical incidents: David's grief at the death of Saul and his son Jonathan (1 Samuel 1.1–12); David's grief for own son Absalom (2 Samuel 18.31–19.2); the Psalms of Lament; the Beatitudes (Matthew 5.4); Jesus at the death of his friend Lazarus (John 11.30–6);

Jesus' concern for the dying daughter of Jairus and the widow of Nain's son; and Jesus' anticipation of his own death.

A belief that has troubled Christians is that of praying for the dead, which can be a great source of comfort to the bereaved particularly to those losing a child, signifying that the child is with a loving and merciful God. Praying for the dead is found in 2 Maccabees 12.41–6, found in Catholic Bibles but not in Protestant Bibles. Anglicans abolished it at the Protestant Reformation (1517–1648), stating it had no scriptural warrant. However, in Westminster Abbey on All Saints' Day, 1919, Archbishop William Temple said in a public sermon:

> Let us pray for those who we know and love who have passed on to the other life... But do not be content to pray for them. Let us also ask them to pray for us. Growth continues beyond the grave and we pray for the dead not because we believe that God will otherwise neglect them, but because we claim the privilege of uniting our love for them with God's. (Wilkinson 1978, p.178)

Another rite is a modified version of the Book of Common Prayer (1928) known as 'Series One' and influenced by the wastage of life in the 1914–1918 War and the subsequent grief. The 1928 Prayer Book introduced alternative Psalms and Scripture readings and new prayers, more than one expressing the belief that Christians could legitimately pray for the dead, or at least for the 'faithful departed'. Series One became authorised in 1967. Praying for the dead has continued to be a problem. Perham believed that the issue was theological, hinging around the question, does the individual come to God's judgement at the moment of death, or not until a final universal judgement (Perham 1997, pp.159–60)? Classic Anglican theology believes that prayer for the dead is improper because at death destiny is settled. Yet the debate continued within Anglicanism, many believing that prayer for the dead was improper. Bishop Ian Ramsay chaired the Doctrine Commission, which attempted an approach for all, 'May God in his infinite love and mercy bring the whole Church, living and departed in the Lord Jesus, to a joyful resurrection and the fulfilment of his eternal kingdom'. This became part of the Alternative Service Book (Church of England 1980) and Common Worship (Church of England 2000). At the funeral service of a child the words used are 'we have come...

to give thanks…to commend him/her to God our merciful redeemer and judge' (Church of England 2000).

For Christians there is the hope of a life beyond this; though this is never spelt out it brings comfort to many in their grieving. Some Christians, such as those of the Salvation Army and those from the Caribbean culture, celebrate death at the funeral with cries of 'Hallelujah'. This needs to be balanced by a time for grief to be expressed.

Christian belief spills over into action. A clear example is that of Sister Frances Dominica, a nun of an Anglican Order, All Saints Sisters of the Poor. Sister Frances was the founder of Helen House Children's Hospice Oxford in 1982, the first hospice for children in the world. It offers respite care and terminal care to children with life-limiting illness, offering friendship and practical help to families that continues after the death of a child for as long as a family needs. Sister Dominica also founded Douglas House in 2004, which offers 'respite' for those between 16 and 40 with life-shortening conditions.

Islam

Islam considers death, 'divinely willed and when it arrives it should be readily accepted' (Opposing Views 2015). Death is considered to be from God (Qur'an 4.78), yet since God is most loving, it must have purpose though we not be able to see it. This may be a reminder in busy human lives that the purpose of life is to worship. Expressing grief is through quiet tears; there is to be no wailing since this can be understood as a rejection of God's will. The body is prepared and bereavement lasts for three days when prayers are recited.

Hinduism

At a death, the body is bathed immediately, often by women. The ritual marks of the community are put on the body while the priest says holy mantras. Flowers are put on the body and rice as food for the soul is put in the mouth and coins in the hand. The body is put on a bier ready for cremation. Children under the age of puberty are buried rather than cremated. The family in a state of grief do not cook until after the cremation; the saying is 'the fire in the house is not lit until the fire in the cremation pyre has gone out'. The ashes of the deceased are taken and scattered in a particular river. After that, friends bring vegetarian food. In the place where the person died a lamp is lit and water provided to light the soul and nourish it on the journey. After the death, there is a period of purification for between 13 and 40 days from pollution, during which time prayers are said and parts of the *Bhagavada Gita* are read. These speak of the soul that never dies and are as the touch of a soothing hand to the bereaved. Gifts of food are given to the poor in memory of the deceased. This is meritorious.

Buddhism

Buddhism understands grief as real, realising our human experience of pain at the death of a loved one. We need to adjust to living without her presence and missing her as part of our lives. The world may seem empty leading to a sense of desperation and feeling sorry for oneself. Yet as we lose, through the death of loved ones we recognise our own mortality and the universality of death. The Buddha explained this, illustrating it by a story. A woman came to the Buddha in anguish carrying in her arms the body of her dead child pleading for the child's return to life. The Buddha said that he would grant her request if she could bring a mustard seed from a household where no one had died. The woman returned a year later having found no such household, realising the universality of death.

Drawing together experience and cultural context leading to practical implications

Childhood is a time of change in physical capacities, in language and in intellectual, emotional, social and spiritual growth; it is not surprising therefore that there are some challenges. Developmental norms help us to know what we might expect of children at different ages, yet growth is varied. Recently, child psychologists have called this holistic growth 'a web' with interacting developments rather than a process of even growth in marked stages. However, in physical development there is a natural sequence; for example, an infant sits and crawls before she walks. Similarly, in conceptual development there are stages as seen in Chapter 1. The emotional and physical reactions to bereavement also show stages. A grieving child needs an adult she loves, respects and feels safe with; this is usually a close relative. If the death is of a parent, this is a threat to the child's whole life and she needs to know that life will continue in some way for her.

The resources of a remaining parent, may be limited as a result of her own grief. The adult needs to be one who respects the child and can recognise that children grieve differently from adults – a person who can receive the child's questions as the child jumps in and out of grief, even when these questions seem callous. Children need to know that grief takes many forms and that it is fine to feel angry, to cry, to sob or to be silent; these are all normal acts of grief. They also need to know that grief continues well after the funeral.

Accepting loss is part of the growth to maturity. Losses, as mentioned in Chapter 1, are many and varied – the physical loss of the first tooth, the loss of childhood at puberty. Helping children and adolescents to confront and learn about loss, grief and bereavement and to develop emotional resources is too important to leave until occasions of personal or public crisis. It is what we make of our losses and how we use them and can grow through loss that matters. In learning how to grieve we are learning skills for life. Children tend to return to a death in a natural way – adults to quit and get on with life. Age-related concepts and behaviours of children and adolescents with an adult response are shown in Table 2.1.

Two useful resources are Heather Butler's (2013) *Helping Children Think About Bereavement: A Differentiated Story and Activities to Help Children Aged 5–11 Deal with Loss,* and *Muddles, Puddles and Sunshine: Your Activity Book to Help When Someone Has Died* (Crossley 2000).

Table 2.1 Age-related concepts and behaviours around death

Age	Concepts	Behaviour	Adult response
A baby/ newborn	No understanding of death, though senses the sadness in the house Concern re. separation	May be signs of irritability, change in eating patterns, disturbed sleep patterns	Normal routines if possible Verbal and physical affection
Toddler	No understanding that death is final and inevitable, though may have some experience of pets dying/seeing a dead bird	Threat to child's world Signs of insecurity: colds, clinging, tantrums, erratic sleep patterns, repeated questions	Consistent care – physical: cuddles; a comforter/ pacifier; books read by carer, messy paints, creative opportunities

cont.

Age	Concepts	Behaviour	Adult response
3–5 yrs/ kinder- garten	Limited understanding of death as sleep so stays awake; or the absence of a parent who works	Affected by parent's emotional state; undermines confidence in world – asks many questions to make sense Clinging; has difficulty verbalising – acts out aggressively, escapes into play Regressive behaviour, bedwetting, thumb sucking	Continuity, routine, reassurance, security, using concrete language, physical affection, reading stories
5–9 yrs	Beginning to accept impermanence and inevitability of death, though it only happens to older people. Fills gaps in understanding with fantasy/magical element	May be afraid of dark, nightmares, regression to baby talk, bedwetting, gaining attention	Talk with child – listen to her concerns Help her share bad dreams demon/ skeleton Model positive – assure that life will go on – will be taken to football/dance lessons Involve in decisions Draw, express grief creatively
9–12 yrs	By ten years most children understand death as universal, irreversible, non functional, i.e. dead things cannot do what living things can Impact of own death Some struggle with death as final possibly because of religious views of afterlife	'Landscape' questions – change is likely e.g. house, new partner or parent Independence Fragile Increased anger and guilt School phobia – bullying Wonders about own death and those around them Anger – why death?	Consistency – Admit when you do not know answers Encourage joining a support group – other youngsters Anticipate mood swings
Adoles- cents	More mature attitudes	Awareness of own mortality – so depression Risk-taking behaviour – drugs, alcohol, fast cars, bikes	These are not yet adults – be there for them Support when needed

ACTIVITIES TO ELICIT THE READER'S EXPERIENCE

Below are three case studies. Respond to the questions from both your own professional experience, and your experience as a mature adult.

Case study 1

Gerald is ten and his father died ten months ago. Gerald lives with his mum and two brothers. He showed no emotion at the funeral, does not talk about his dad, and if others speak of him, he leaves the room. His mum has become concerned because Gerald is not achieving at school; he is withdrawn and losing friends.

- Why do you feel Gerald is reacting this way?

- How do you think Gerald could be helped and supported with his loss?

Case study 2

David is five. His mother, Anne, died recently after being ill for many months. Often when his mother was very poorly or in hospital, David would stay with his grandma, since his dad worked long hours. His grandma lives some distance away. After one visit to Grandma he did not see his mother again. David didn't ask where his mother was and Grandma has suggested to David's dad that all photos of Anne should be put away in case they remind David of his mother. Recently David has begun to say he can see 'Mummy'.

- Why do you feel David is reacting in this way?

- How do you think he could be supported in his loss?

Case study 3

Jason was eight when his mum died. His parents were separated yet seemed to be beginning to understand one another again. Mum had dropped Jason off at school as usual and later that morning had been killed in a car accident. That evening his dad picked him up from school, which was very unusual, and took him to his nan's where Dad was living. They told Jason what had happened to his mum. He asked lots of questions to find out things and tried to imagine his mother and the accident. Dad took him back to Jason's home and picked up some clothes before returning him to Nan's. Nan did not think it was suitable for children to go to funerals, but Dad asked his work mate who had lost his wife and he said it was OK. So Jason went. He did not like talking about what had happened to his mum for fear of upsetting his nan and dad. His dad was worried about him since

Jason was so quiet. Jason would spend long periods in his bedroom at his nan's and one day Dad heard him crying.

- Why do you think Jason was so quiet?
- What could Dad do to help?
- What long-term solutions might help in this situation?

The questions in these case studies can be tackled using the process model shown in the figure below.

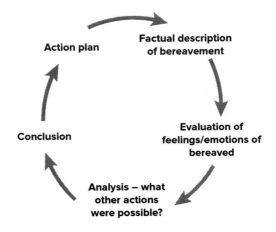

3

Challenging Factors Influencing Grief

It's just goodness and happiness and warm.
(Cameron writing about heaven, Marshall 2003, p.23)

A child's experience

The smoke alarm in the hospice was set off following Janice's visit to the chapel. She had lit all the tealight candles in the bowl of sand available for anyone to light as rising prayers to God. She lit them as prayers for her dad, who was a patient in the hospice suffering the last stages of Parkinson's disease.

Reflection on experience

Many people would think this a desperate and pointless action – Janice felt the only thing she could do was pray since she was fearful of losing her beloved father. Visiting the hospice regularly, Janice had noticed her dad getting worse. Now he could no longer walk though he had been a keen football player, and his speech was unclear. Janice longed for his healing. Healing can mean many things including freedom from pain; some believe that death is the ultimate healing as a release from pain.

An adolescent's experience

Sandra was 14 and in her public examinations year. She was very sensitive and such a caring girl that other girls came to her with their problems. Some girls, perhaps out of jealousy, bullied her. Eventually life became too much for Sandra, and she wrote in her journal that she wanted to end it all. A friend happened to see the journal and, worried by its content, reported it to their form teacher. The head teacher was told and called for a meeting as soon as possible with the school counsellor and Sandra, whose mother was then informed. The mother came to the school greatly distressed. Sandra met the counsellor and warmed to her, finding their conversation helpful. The father was telephoned and was furious that the school were interfering and said that this was a family affair

Reflection on experience

The school acted quickly since the staff and particularly the counsellor were trained in the volatile behaviour of adolescents. They know the signs when all is not well with a pupil and had measures to deal with this in Sandra's case. However, in the case of a minor, parents must be involved, particularly in this instance where the attitudes of mother and father were very different. In the ongoing care of Sandra it was necessary to see her father. The head teacher arranged to see him at home, on his own territory, to help him understand that while it was a family affair, it was helpful to Sandra to work with someone outside the family whose expertise was adolescence and who maintained strict confidentiality.

The link of adult, child and adolescent experience

Children and adolescents are much more 'hands on' than adults. They take action and do the practical thing in the present moment. Janice expressed her grief about the possibility of losing her father by lighting all the tealight candles in the chapel as a prayer to God. Sandra was practical in that she wrote a journal in which to record her thoughts including what she might do in the future. Adults tend to ruminate and think carefully. In the examples in this chapter we address difficult situations affecting children and adolescents where adults do not always recognise the implications for them. For example following a miscarriage or a stillbirth, siblings will feel the pain of loss but their grief can be ignored. There are other situations, such as the terminal illness of a parent with young children, when there are long-lasting repercussions for the wellbeing of the children. Often it is thought that they don't understand as much as adults involved.

Sociological, psychological and historical insights to factors influencing grief

Models of grief were discussed in Chapter 2 and these refer to normal grief. While recognising the variety within normal grief, and an overlap between normal and complicated grief, the latter has distinctive features. Difficulties in complicated grief are conceptualised in terms of the grief process and the 'tasks of grieving' following a complicated death.

Difficulties in the grief process are considered to be:

- the absence of grief after a major bereavement

- delayed grief, when the bereaved delays beginning a grief process and later is overwhelmed

- inhibited grief, that is grief that is limited

- unbalanced grief, since the bereaved is grieving but appears stuck in one emotion

- chronic grief, because the bereaved appears stuck in one particular phase of grief.

The tasks of grieving following a complicated death are as follows:

- *Task 1*: The reality of the loss has not been fully acknowledged.

- *Task 2*: The bereaved has not allowed himself to experience the pain of loss.

- *Task 3*: The bereaved is unable to adjust to living without the deceased.

- *Task 4*: The bereaved is unable to let go and does not have the energy to go forward and rebuild a life for himself.

Conceptualising grief in these two ways helps in knowing what responses are possible.

Certain factors make grief more likely to be difficult, though this is not always the case:

- A first factor is the nature of the death: uncertainty of death – for example, the disappearance of someone while swimming but no body is found; unnatural death, such as murder, terrorism, soldiers in war zones; sudden unexpected death; multiple deaths in a road accident; death accompanied by other losses; suicide.

- A second factor is the nature of the relationship of the bereaved with the deceased. Was this a dependent relationship, such as that between a baby and a mother; an extremely close relationship such as parent and child; or an ambivalent relationship between adolescent and parent? The nature of the relationship will indicate the grief, though it must be recognised that each bereavement is unique.

- A third factor is the nature and circumstances of the bereaved person: their age; their psychological strength; how they coped with previous losses; the presence of other stresses, such as financial worries; social support; the presence of a close friend to share confidences; idiosyncratic needs and cultural differences.

These three factors will now be applied in several particular situations with indications of how grief is addressed.

Miscarriage, stillbirths and cot deaths

A hundred years ago the death of a child was commonplace, as was that of a woman in childbirth. Today in the West these events are rarer but stillbirths and cot deaths do occur and adults may feel outrage and anger such that even humanists might turn to say that God did nothing to prevent the death, appearing powerless to intervene. Sadly in Britain the death of a baby is not uncommon; a quarter of pregnancies do not end with a live birth. In the UK each day 17 women experience a stillbirth (James 2004, p.136). In 2012 stillbirths were 4 per cent of live births, the lowest figure ever. This is still an unacceptably high level and this necessitates an emphasis and a political will to pay for research into the reasons for stillbirth. In 2013, 2767 babies under a year old died.

An article about Laura's stillbirth brought responses of silence. Her mother, Alice, wrote, 'We live in a society that is in denial about death. Get the dead under the sod with the minimum of fuss and move on to the next thing straight-away. That's the current approach' (Jolly 2007, p.3). The contrast is made with the mourning rituals of the Victorians and today Italian and Spanish graveyards with their photographs and the importance other countries attach to All Souls Day (see Chapter 7). Laura's parents already had a son and a month after Laura's stillbirth, he had his third birthday. Alice said, 'My son's questions went on and on. Do people come alive again? How will my sister grow if she's in the ground? Can we buy a new baby?' Young children need to make sense of a death in their own way, expressing their grief through questioning, although this is very difficult for a mother alongside her own feelings of grief. There is help for grieving mothers, and Alice found it through the community sharing of those who had similarly lost a baby, in the Stillbirth and Neonatal Death Society (SANDS).

Mothers suffering a miscarriage, stillbirth, cot death or the termination of a pregnancy may have a specialist midwife to support and facilitate culturally and spiritually appropriate care. The baby may be washed and dressed; hand and footprints taken and a lock of hair cut and preserved; there may be photographs. The challenge is giving a mother choice by asking in a way that is not offensive, but right for her. Chaplains may 'bless' dead babies and say prayers for the baby, with or without parents present, which may be helpful for the grieving mother and her wider family and friendship network; this may also include naming the child. Some mothers prefer not to name a baby; an example is the case with mothers of African heritage 'as naming is something that happened days after the birth and has its own cultural and religious pattern' (Rhodes 2013, p.132). There may be a religious or non-religious ceremony to acknowledge the death when parents talk of their hopes for and feelings about what might have been had the baby lived. Chaplains may give a 'blessing card to affirm the reality of a child and offer something to remember it by, in a place where there perhaps seems little to hold on to' (Rhodes 2013, p.133). Hospices and hospitals may offer memorial services. All these actions of care are significant in a traumatic experience, for the mother in particular, but also the father or partner.

In Alice Jolly's situation, her three-year-old son persisted with questions about her miscarriage, questions which were very relevant and natural for his age but difficult for her to handle. Parents may find explanations difficult. There can be a tendency to forget the siblings of 'a baby to be' who may be traumatised. It can be that the life of a sibling may be dominated by memories of the baby who died. (See the example of Jamie whose early life was dominated by the death of a twin sister in Chapter 7.) Stories that can be used with children include *Goodbye Baby: Cameron's Story* (Griffiths and Mcleod 2010), a book to read with young children who have known about a mother's miscarriage, and *The Very Hungry Caterpillar,* a story of transformation in nature (Carle 2002).

A child with a terminal illness

The news that a baby is born with a life-threatening illness requiring constant medical attention is one of the hardest events that a couple or a parent face. It can cost a marriage. The feelings of guilt and anger may dominate at first, followed by living with the uncertainty and having to continue life while adjusting to a new situation. The siblings of the child may be affected through picking up parental emotions. For some there is a feeling of what might have been and a period of anticipatory grief – grief before a death, but one that progresses through the 'normal' stages of grief. In this situation the parent's grief is profound, shattering life, since no parent expects to pre-decease their child; it does not seem natural. Yet approximately six thousand children a year die in the UK. Many grieving adults find it very difficult to talk about the illness and likely death to friends, family or even each other. Winston's Wish comments, 'this can sometimes cause strain. However, it can also be helpful if you (parents) have different strategies and ideas that might work for each other at different times' (Winston's Wish 2001, p.6).

David Cameron and his wife Samantha's first child, Ivan, was born with severe epilepsy and cerebral palsy. Samantha reflected on their realisation that something was wrong with Ivan saying, 'It's your worst nightmare. They did a lot of tests, you go into the office with the doctor and they push the box of tissues towards you and you feel like you're in an episode of *Casualty*' (a British hospital 'soap' TV series). She later said:

> It changes your life for ever. It's tough, lonely and isolating initially. You're living in a completely different world to your friends who've had babies at the same time. You're suddenly in this weird world of doctors and social services. You know your child is never going to meet the normal milestones. (Prince 2015)

They knew Ivan's life span was limited and for six years he was in and out of hospital. During that time the Camerons had two other children, Nancy and Arthur. His sister and brother did not seem to perceive Ivan's disability as making him different from them.

Ivan died on 25 February 2009, aged six. Nancy was then five and Arthur was three. Ivan's sudden loss was heart breaking for them as well as for David and Samantha. His siblings will find it difficult to understand what has happened to Ivan and they will wonder where Ivan has gone and when he is coming back.

The emotional rollercoaster of parents with a baby born with a severe defect, or exposed to disease which becomes life threatening or an accident, is devastating. Working with a child with a life-threatening illness is especially demanding. Care is about dispelling guilt in both child and parent, honesty, open answers, listening to the child's understanding of the illness, showing love, offering security and explaining in a language the child can understand. The sick child suffers, but so do the child's siblings, perhaps because, almost inevitably, most of the available time is focused on the sick child.

Sister Frances, in charge of St Helen's Children's Hospice, tells of an incident with two brothers: Harry aged six and his five-year-old brother Cameron. They had grown up together and played together. Now Harry was on a syringe driver in the Children's Hospice.

Cameron spent part of each day with his brother. His brother had to be told of the seriousness of Harry's condition and while he played in the corridor, Sister Frances knelt beside him and told him that his brother was going to die in the next day or two.

> Cameron looked as if he'd been hit by something that had knocked all the air out of him and then he carried on playing. The news had to sink in slowly... I felt as though I had taken away his innocence and something died in me too... Cameron was out of the room when Harry died the following day, but we brought him in immediately and he said his own goodbyes. His shock was indescribable but totally visible – it hurt me to the core to see Cam suffering like this, but I knew I couldn't shelter him from it, just as no one could save us from the pain either. (The Guild of St Raphael, Children's Hospice 2002)

Bereavement support is offered to parents and siblings of a child who dies and a child whose parent dies by organisations such as Children's Hospices and websites. In the USA there is an organisation called 'Bereaved Parents', a national self-help group offering support, understanding, compassion and hope to bereaved parents, grandparents and siblings struggling to rebuild their lives after the death of their children or grandchildren. It holds monthly support meetings called 'chapters' and produces a newsletter and brochures (see the Useful Websites and Organisations section).

The sudden death of a child

A sudden death may happen as a result of an accident or undetected illness. The latter was the case with Tom who died in his sleep on Friday 5 October 2007. His father, Paul, found him and called the ambulance. As an unexpected death the police became involved and arrived at the home. Tom's sister, a year younger, was at school; she realised that it was bad news when she was taken unexpectedly out of class. On Monday the coroner called stating that Tom had died from an extremely rare heart condition and that nothing could have predicted it nor anything been done to prevent it. The funeral was a celebration of Tom's life at which his sister spoke through her tears. His father commented on grief, 'Life carries on with a Tom-shaped hole in its fabric. Sometimes it rips further, sometimes it's less frayed, but it's always there...when your child is cut from your life you bleed and keep on bleeding.' The effect on his thirteen-year-old daughter must have been immense. He says of her:

> Ellen, meanwhile, is both my greatest hope and my greatest fear. Hope because I now see a young woman who appears, despite everything, to be a rounded human being. Sure, she's spent her teenage years discovering booze, fags and goodness knows what else, but she seems to have done this in a way all teenagers do. Fear because who knows what goes on in somebody's head, especially that of your own teenage daughter? It's not the easiest or most communicative of ages. Do I just see what I long to see? However, we think we dealt with Tom's death as parents, (she) will have a different perspective. I simply hope for the best. (Clabburn 2013, pp.30–31)

Paul felt the pain and agony of Tom's death. In the death of a child, if the pain of grief is blocked, harm is done. Jim would not hear the name of his teenage daughter spoken after she was killed in a car accident, neither has he ever mentioned her name. He refused the help and counselling available. His daughter's death has changed his character and his relationship with a younger daughter, whose grief is also blocked by his attitude. Pain can be blocked by silence, or as for Jim, by drugs, drink and sex.

Friends and family want to help the bereaved parents cheer up, but this does not help, neither do easy answers nor platitudes such as, 'She was like a beautiful flower and God wanted her for His garden.' It is important to give the bereaved plenty of time and opportunities to say what they really feel; to be available; to accept the story of the death repeated again and again. Sometimes there is the anger of guilt: the father who didn't see his child and backed his car, killing her. Guilt is an emotion that gnaws inside if not addressed; expert help may be needed – if the person is religious a sympathetic priest may help. Listening to the bereaved frees them to be themselves at whatever stage they are. In some situations, sympathetic touch is appropriate. The death of a child is never forgotten by a parent but remembered through photographs, carried within memories and in the heart. There is also a danger that such a death and its ensuing grief can blight the lives of the siblings of the deceased who themselves will be expressing grief, though their grief is different.

A child who has a terminally ill parent

If the family can cope the best place to die is at home. However, statistics show that 53 per cent of terminally ill people die in hospital compared with 21 per cent at home (see Chapter 3). Reasons for a final hospitalisation and death are varied. They include the distress of the family, who cannot cope now and don't want to continue to live in the house where the parent died; lack of room to provide privacy to the sick parent; or a family's fear of being ill equipped to deal with medications. The gain from being at home is the opportunity during the illness to get together as a family and share what has happened during the day, school activities, the doctor's visit, memories of past happy times and times to come. It can also be relaxing together as a family, maybe each tea time, simply enjoying the positive things that have happened. Constant visits from professionals, friends and distant family can be intrusive to the ordinary routine of family life, but this is not ordinary time. Children can feel left out and need specific chores to do for which they are responsible, as part of a carefully ordered routine. It is important that illness does not take over the family life. A partner as a carer needs to recharge batteries; maybe a friendly neighbour can sit with a sick mother, while Dad and the children go out together and have a short break.

Using the illustration of a wife and mother dying as an example, gradually a father will spend more time caring and have less time with his children so he will need others to help with the household chores. These may be extended family, neighbours, other professionals or a social services carer. At this time children may notice a change of identity in the sick parent: Mum, once seemingly omnipotent and who could do anything – make breakfast, eat it and create packed lunches while having conversations about the need of clothes for a gym lesson – now cannot stand to do jobs and they have to be done one at a time gradually. Janice, who lit all the candles in the chapel, had noticed the deterioration in her father's health and condition; for her, he had changed. In the future there may be a stepmother who has not been part of the relationship with the child during a period of their life when the children have experienced emotional turmoil.

For some sick parents there is a desire themselves to prepare for their children's future lives without them. Violet was concerned about her grandchildren who were young – too young to understand the idea of death's finality. Violet wanted to write a letter to be given to them after her death. She wanted to assure her grandchildren that death was something positive and not frightening. She thought of her grandchildren's fun on the slide in the park; death was like this, there was the effort of climbing to the top of the slide and then the excitement and freedom of letting go and sliding down. This was a letter her grandchildren would want to keep and treasure. Anne decided to write a letter to each of her daughters to open on their eighteenth birthdays. This said how proud she was of the child, now an adult, and that she was still close to them and always would be in their memories. Anne thought about a present that could be given to her daughters after her death: a necklace for each with a heart-shaped case which could contain a small photo of her. Dan, her husband, helped her in this. These actions were a solace to Anne's teenage daughters and showed them that she had continued to love and think about them when she was dying.

In the hospice, family support staff helped terminally ill patients choose, make and fill memory boxes for their children and grandchildren. These contained a variety of things such as a lock of hair, the remnants of a favourite bottle of perfume, a recorded message and photos of the family holidays. They were a comfort to families after the death; some families keep the boxes in special places and bring them out on significant occasions, such as the anniversary of the death, and may add other pieces of memory. For some patients, however, making a memory box was beyond their ability in accepting the possibility of their death.

Some terminally parents die in a hospital or hospice. Visiting times in hospitals are limited but there is usually a lounge from which children can come and go from Mum's bed, which is useful for a young child's short attention span. Older children can be encouraged to take homework to do and Mum might be well enough to take an interest and help. A young child can rearrange the greetings cards, draw a card or tidy the bedside cabinet. However parents may be reluctant to allow children to go to the hospital for fear of what else a child might see, particularly in oncology wards where people are very ill and may be hooked up to a variety of machines.

Ana Draper is a Macmillan consultant specialised in working with families facing a life-threatening illness and the author of *Good Grief: What Will We Tell the Kids?* (Draper 2008). Sensitivity is central to the care of children with a parent who has a life-threatening illness. Ana recommends listening to children and asking them whether they want to ask anything. Usually the child knows intuitively what is happening but sometimes a conspiracy of silence prevails. On occasions there is a half-truth told to children. Amy, a seven-year-old, was told by her maternal grandmother that her mother who was dying at home with cancer was getting better. When her mother died a few days later, Amy's anger was significant. We maintain silence because we think that childhood innocence should not be broken, and children should be free from difficult and challenging life events. Many parents want to protect their child when one of them is terminally ill, but it is more helpful to talk about the progress of the illness so that children feel included in what is happening.

In these difficult circumstances of a terminal illness, adults worry about what to say, saying the wrong thing to children or being asked questions they feel they can't answer (see Chapter 4). When children want to know, answer them realistically, honestly and frankly, without recourse to euphemisms; the result will be that trust continues to build between adult and child. The support services such as the Macmillan and hospice nurses need to work in parallel with parents and the schools that children attend. A child's need for information or choice not to talk should be respected. It is important to consult children and to involve them in decisions so that they can recover some sense of control in a world that has suddenly been turned upside down.

For children facing the imminent death of a parent and challenging grief experiences, it is about working with them, perhaps in play using appropriate media such as puppets, books and creativity, discovering from the child what he knows and wants to know. It is important to respond to children honestly for young children are matter of fact; they also soon forget and will ask again. A book which may help is a Winston's Wish publication, *As Big As It Gets*, which contains ideas to help parents and carers to involve their children in what is happening when a parent is seriously ill (Winston's Wish 2007).

When the death happens, in some ways it can be a relief for the child. Care after the death will continue through support at the funeral. For the father losing a child suddenly, for example through an undetected condition (usually a heart attack), a downloadable booklet for bereaved fathers at the Cardiac Risk in the Young website may help with bereavement support (see the Useful Websites and Organisations section).

Tragic events: reaction to the events of 9/11 in New York

The total killed in the bombing of the Twin Towers in New York was 2823. These included employees in the Towers, firefighters, paramedics, police and Port Authority police officers. There were 161 families with no remains to grieve (Templeton and Lumley 2002). Many of those who died left children. Those who died came from 115 nations making it, in this sense, an act of indiscriminate bombing. These figures come from a year after the disaster when the psychological stress, trauma, anxiety and depression continued.

Children heard the news in the UK from shocked parents at the school gates. At home those who had family and friends in New York wanted to check that they were safe. Children saw in the media the repeats of planes flown into the two towers resulting in the death of many. Children cannot be shielded from such events which dominate the media. At school the following morning head teachers acknowledged what had happened and expressed the sadness of the loss of life. Children were encouraged to talk openly in response to the event. The younger children, who tend to 'puddle jump', moved from sadness at an event in which they were not personally involved to getting on with life. Grant, age 11, rationalised, 'It was a cruel thing to do, but they only do it because they are sick and selfish' (Duffy 2008, p.12). Most of the youngsters were outraged as they watched the TV in horror. Adolescents might discuss the implications of some of the events, for example that these so-called 'terrorist' attacks are often indiscriminate in their victims, particularly their nationality. Contacts with the local Muslim community and a visit to a local mosque and discussion there might help.

Children and adolescents are affected by tragic events even when, for those in the UK, these are far from their own homes. Adolescents can identify with the emotions of grief of others and the anger of an unprovoked action. In the UK on the 7 July 2005 terrorist bombs killed 52 in London and injured more than 700. Services were held on the tenth anniversary in 2015 marking the 'ocean of pain'. More recently there was an accident with the loss of six lives, with 15 others badly injured in Glasgow when a bin lorry crashed on 22 December 2014. The media headlines cannot be avoided by children.

Soldiers killed on duty

Soldiers often have families. These deaths are taken seriously by the military and funerals given honour, since those dying in these situations have died while working for their country. Families are helped by the annual Remembrance Day parade and service when the dead are honoured and children participating realise that they are not alone in their grief. Winston's Wish have a book to support bereaved children in this situation: *The Family Has Been Informed* (see the Useful Websites and Resources section).

Murder

When it is children who are abducted and murdered, as happened to Holly Wells and Jessica Chapman in 2001 in Soham, Cambridgeshire, their close friends show bewilderment, confusion and fear. Duffy commented:

> they may have shown anxiety at being separated from parents… perhaps fear of the dark and of having nightmares. They will have felt vulnerable for a while, afraid something of the same could happen to them – feeling jumpy or 'spooked' as they read 'danger' into ordinary sights and sounds. (Duffy 2008, p.48)

When tragic events happen and our children and adolescents become fearful, parents and teachers must listen and help them to understand. Adults need to be realistic, since there are individuals who perpetrate terrible acts, but they also need to reassure children that these events are not the norm; there is a great deal of kindness and truth in the world and the adults in their lives love and care for them. Winston's Wish publications have produced a book for youngsters called *Hope Beyond the Headlines* (see the Useful Websites and Resources section).

Suicide

In the past, if the person who died by suicide was known to a child, there was pressure not to tell the child that they had taken their own life. This could be because adults find it difficult to understand the motives of someone who dies by suicide, and we do not know how to explain the event to a child. There is a tendency to say that the person died in an accident or that the person has gone away, but in the long run the truth will come out. If a child is not told they may hear the news from someone else, or an adult or another child will let it slip by accident or teasing: 'I know what happened to your mum.' Sometimes when children are not told they may feel that the suicide was somehow their fault, that they caused the death; they fill in the gaps in their knowledge with their imagination and feel guilt.

If the person who died is very close to a child, for example a parent or an older sibling, then explanations are difficult but must be addressed, since the grieving emotions are manifold. Winston's Wish suggests that a parent could say something like: 'I have something to tell you. It's something that has made me feel very sad and at first I didn't know what I was going to say to you. But it's something you need to know. Yesterday John died.' It adds that:

> It's important that children understand what has happened and although details can seem painful and unnecessary, children often need to know what happened, why and how it happened and what happens next. It helps to give children clear facts rather than complicated words. (Winston's Wish 2001, p.10)

Children are profoundly affected by a devastating grief; emotions may include guilt, and self-blame. Sometimes, for an adolescent, if the parent had a history of alcoholism, depression or sexual abuse then there may be a sense of relief that this experience of life is over, but quickly guilt and remorse fill the gap because of the initial sense of relief. A child may fear that the surviving parent will take the same action causing insecurity and mistrust, and an adolescent may question, 'When I am older, will I do the same?' The best person to talk to a child and work with his grief is the surviving parent, but his own grief may make this impossible to bear. However, this difficult grief needs addressing for the child and adolescent and it is sometimes possible for another member of the family to help or someone outside that family such as a close neighbour, a teacher or school counsellor.

It is significant to realise that until 1961 suicide was a crime in the UK, and a failed attempt warranted a prison sentence. The Church would not bury a suicide victim in consecrated ground. Fortunately our understanding has largely changed and we are more sympathetic to a person who attempts suicide, though old ideas still linger. The Alliance of Hope for Suicide Survivors states that according to World Health Organization statistics, approximately one million people die by suicide annually (see the Useful Websites and Organisations section). In the UK a range of support for those affected by a death by suicide is offered by SOBS, Survivors of Bereavement by Suicide.

Well at School is a website maintained and developed by Chelsea Community Hospital School in conjunction with teachers, hospital schools and health care professionals. It produces resources for use in schools on general medical and mental health including signs of depression in adolescents and self-harm, which may be a   physical manifestation of a deep emotional problem. For parents worried about their children and dying people's mental health the YoungMinds 'Save the Parents' helpline is a useful resource (see Useful Websites and Organisations).

A further useful resource for young children is *Luna's Red Hat: An Illustrated Storybook to Help Children Cope with Loss and Suicide* (Smid 2015). The book also includes a guide for parents and professionals by grief expert, Dr Riet Fiddelaers-Jaspers. The book tells of a beautiful spring day, and Luna is having a picnic in the park with her family, wearing her Mum's red hat. Luna's mum died one year ago and she still finds it difficult to understand why. She feels that it may have been her fault and worries that her dad might leave her in the same way. Her dad talks to her to explain what happened and together they think about all the happy memories they have of Mum. This is a tool to be read with children aged six years and above. The author of *Luna's Red Hat* had a schoolmate who died by suicide when they were both 16. At 21 her aunt died by suicide leaving daughters aged 11 and 14. Winston's Wish has a book called *Beyond the Rough Rock* giving practical advice for families and professionals in the immediate days and weeks following a suicide; the book includes child-friendly activities (see the Useful Websites and Resources section).

Children and adolescents who die by suicide

Statistics on the suicides of children and adolescents are hard to find. The latest details from the Office of National Statistics relates to 2009 when 952 males and 534 females died by suicide aged 5–34 years. In 2011 the YoungMinds organisation reported 194 suicides of 15–19-year-olds. Articles in Patient Plus are written by UK doctors and are based on research evidence, UK and European Guidelines (see the Useful Websites and Organisations section). This source suggests depression as an increased risk of suicide, with risk factors ranging from family discord; bullying; physical, sexual or emotional abuse; a history of parental depression; homelessness; refugee status; and living in institutional settings. Ritalin may be prescribed by GPs which may help temporarily but does not get to the root of the problem.

Children and adolescents may display sadness and helplessness, feel unloved and unfairly treated and have a poor self-image. One outcome is poor eating and playing with food. Management is through support and listening by someone confidential outside the family, perhaps a teacher or a school nurse. Later if behaviour does not improve there may be a need to approach a child psychologist. For adolescents, behavioural symptoms include use of drugs, erratic behaviour, insomnia and feelings of guilt and despair. Assessment is particularly difficult with adolescents, since questions may be answered with silence, and young people can be manipulative and therefore require a second opinion. Self-harm can be regarded as a form of communication and is not always picked up. It is sometimes difficult to decipher the adolescent's exact intentions. Deliberate self-harm is common in adolescents, especially females, and there should be an immediate referral. Management of an adolescent client must be taken seriously through referral to paediatricians, social workers or teachers trained in counselling. Suggested techniques include cognitive behaviour therapy and anti-depressants, though the latter can increase risk of self-harm and attempting suicide. Teachers need to be alert and act with others when there are distinct behavioural changes in a child or adolescent, since parents may be unaware of the situation. The increase in self-harm in children and adolescents needs an urgent response.

Babies and infants dying

Infants born pre-term who struggle to survive, or those born with congenital abnormalities or suffering from birthing difficulties, such as lack of oxygen, bring emotional pain and challenge to parents and paediatricians. In the past the doctors – parents were not consulted – fed and kept the baby warm, while allowing nature to take its course. Death usually resulted. Today many paediatricians make strenuous efforts to help the infant survive, though he may be disabled or have a limited life span, while others are beginning to advocate infant/child euthanasia.

The Netherlands

In late 2000, the Dutch parliament voted to legalise euthanasia for adults suffering extreme pain and with no hope of recovery. Between 1997 and 2004 there were 10–15 cases of infant euthanasia a year, but only one fifth were reported, due to doctors fearing a murder charge. After decades of discussion, guidelines were written by Eduard Verhagen, head of the Department of Paediatrics at the University Medical Centre, Groningen. In 2005 the Netherlands recognised this 'Groningen Protocol' as the set of criteria outlining the circumstances making it permissible to end the life of a baby under the age of one.

Euthanasia can only be undertaken if an infant's diagnosis and prognosis are certain and confirmed by an independent doctor; there is evidence of hopeless and unbearable suffering; both parents give their consent; the procedure follows medical standards and all details are documented (Verhagen and Saucer 2005).

Since 2005, there have been only two cases of euthanasia, the decline correlating with an increase in late terminations, up to the 24th week of pregnancy, particularly in cases of spina bifida. Since 2007, free ultrasound scans have been offered at 20 weeks when the condition can be detected, severity determined and, in some cases, surgery is possible. If the condition is severe, mothers are able decide to terminate or continue the pregnancy; most decide to terminate.

In June 2015, the Dutch Paediatric Association asked for the current age limit of 12 years for the right to die to be considered arbitrary, so that each child under the age of 12 who asks to die will be evaluated on a case-by-case basis. Verhagen stated that if a child under 12 satisfies the conditions outlined above, euthanasia was an option; paediatricians are currently powerless to help and it was time to change. The Association want a commission set up to examine the question further. Euthanasia remains technically illegal for children under 12, however doctors are not prosecuted if the Protocol's criteria are met (Nuwer 2014).

Belgium

Euthanasia was decriminalised for the terminally ill over 18 years old in 2002 and for some infant euthanasia seemed the logical next step. There were paediatricians on both sides of the debate, many signed an open letter against any law, claiming that modern medicine was capable of alleviating pain. They warned of a slippery slope where very sick children could be pressured into choosing death. From the dominant Roman Catholic church there were religious and ethical arguments against any law. In 2014, the Belgian Parliament faced these challenges and gave children the opportunity, in exceptional circumstances, to choose the time and nature of their death allowing euthanasia for terminally ill babies and children without any age limit, by 86 votes to 44 with 12 abstentions (BBC News 2014). Belgium was the first country in the world to pass a law allowing a terminally ill child to choose euthanasia. The law has strict checks. The child must request euthanasia on several occasions; be in a terminal condition; be in constant, unbearable pain that cannot be alleviated by medication; they must understand the meaning of 'euthanasia' and be assessed by a psychiatrist to ensure they understand the implications of their decision; parents and doctors must agree to the request. If there is any doubt that the decision to die is not the child's, doctors err on the side of life.

The challenge is whether or not a child has the capacity to make the judgement to live or die. Does the decision place an inappropriate burden of responsibility on a child? Tom Riddington, a doctor, wrote a response to the Belgian decision in *The Guardian* newspaper, noting that:

> the new law at least allows a discussion to take place, without fear of legal repercussions. It gives parents and children a chance to know all the options available... For the terminally ill child, their parents and their doctors, this dilemma is a daily reality. (Riddington 2014)

The UK

In 2005, the Nuffield Council of Bioethics launched an enquiry into critical care in fetal and neonatal medicine, and the ethical, social and legal issues which might arise when making decisions surrounding treatment (Nuffield Council on Bioethics 2005). The Royal College of Obstetricians and Gynaecologists submitted a recommendation that a public debate be started on options of 'non-resuscitation, withdrawal of treatment decisions, the best interests, tests and active euthanasia' for 'the sickest of newborns.' The College stated that there should be discussion over whether 'deliberate intervention' to cause death to severely disabled newborn babies should be legalised. While it was not necessarily in favour of the move, it felt the issues should be debated (Royal College of Obstetricians and Gynaecologists 2005).

Details of this argument and ethical implications can be found in Appendix 4.

Believers' experiences – world faiths

Judaism

The traditional rule is that standard mourning practices do not apply to a child (or, by extension, a foetus) that does not survive until the thirty-first day after birth. This seemingly harsh rule arose from the high rate of neonatal mortality that prevailed universally well into the Victorian era. Today with differing streams within Judaism, traditional Jews may still follow the old laws. But increasingly Jews will follow mourning practices for a stillborn or neonatal death to a greater or lesser extent as they find appropriate or comforting in the same way as for any other death. Since there are no rules, it is up to individuals in their own circumstances, and in consonance with the local community's practices, to do what they find appropriate. Mourning for an aborted foetus is similar. The ceremonies for a child that lives more than 30 days are the same as for any other person.

A resource that may be used in response to difficult death is the Psalms of Lament in the Hebrew Scriptures, shared by both Jews and Christians. For example:

> Rouse yourself! Why do you sleep, O Lord?
> Awake, do not cast us off forever!
> Why do you hide your face?
> Why do you forget our affliction and oppression?
> For we sink down to the dust; our bodies cling to the ground.
> Rise up, come to our help.
> Redeem us for the sake of your steadfast love.
>
> (Psalm 44.23–6)

These psalms provide insights that could illuminate the human condition.

They are a Theology of Vulnerable Presence; after the anger which may follow a loss, there may be a time of waiting, which cannot be bypassed. This giving of unhurried, supportive, acceptance of emotions is a God-like characteristic.

Christianity

Suffering has challenged belief in an omnipotent and loving God. The question of how to justify God in the face of innocent suffering – theodicy – has been the domain of philosophers and theologians for centuries. Omnipotence is not a description of God's being, rather it is a veto against the apparent reality that not God, but suffering and death, wield ultimate power in the world. Research findings and a recommendation can be found in relation to children in Korneck (2012). It relates to Germany where religious education is taught in state schools. 'Theology for and by children' has recently received debate and academic interest. Children, like adults, ask ultimate questions about the reason for suffering and the final meaning of life, often being more radical than adults since they are not impressed by complicated philosophy. Most teachers agree that asking questions is the most important methodological tool for the task. Children experience suffering in may ways: through an increasing number living in poverty; suffering illness, particularly chronic illness; suffering inadequate or absent relationships; living in an environment that fills them with fear; and the awareness that their future is being threatened (Oberthur 2006, pp.44–45). Yet in Children's Bibles the image is of a nice God, omitting the reality of evil and fear which children experience in their lives.

> To talk about God as the one who is in control of hopeless situations and who is able to turn them around is an important task that we are not allowed to avoid by simply hiding the misery. Children will, and justifiably so – when they are becoming older at least – classify biblical stories as meaningless and 'childish' if they are not able to describe their reality comprehensively or even just euphemistically. In the stories that cause fear, children take part in the whole range of human experience, which people in the Old Testament have made with God and which children already know, based on their everyday life. (Korneck in Lawson 2012, p.429)

Stories of fear that are cited include the flood, the sacrifice of Isaac and the Exodus from Egypt. The Old Testament is full of an angry God, for example Psalms 10, 88 and 137, yet God is seen on the side of the weak, poor and oppressed and, in the history of Israel's suffering, God takes away the fear of dying.

> [A discussion] with a first grade class in primary school with incessant input by the pupils on the topic 'always against the little' made obvious…how especially the topic 'violence towards weaker people' is relevant among children…they have a very clear understanding of the fact that violence can proceed from them i.e. they can be victims as well as offenders, they…told about incidents, in which the first grade was maltreated by the fourth graders or about conflicts among siblings…would we fade out biblical texts that contain violence for children, we would once again take away possibilities of identification with situations in their life we would not be able to prevent them from experiencing anyway. (Korneck in Lawson 2012, p.430)

The research was done using a survey of twelve rural and urban primary schools in North West Germany. Children were asked to state, 'What I would ask God…' and given no guidance. The 2634 responses were analysed and classified according to strict categories. The result showed the deep need in primary education to ask theological questions, and as children grew older the question of suffering and theodicy occurred more and more. More than 56 per cent of all questions concerned suffering. The response was to advocate Children's Bibles containing the story of Job. Job is a story which handles suffering, fear, sorrow and doubt with Job, like children, challenging God to respond and change the situation. For me the answer is an acknowledgement of the mystery of life and God through those wonderful chapters on creation (Job 36.24–41.34) and Job's repentance (42.1–6) and his final restoration (42.7–17). The researcher's conclusion is that talking with children about the book of Job avoids creating barriers for children with readymade answers.

> We cannot leave children alone when they search for answers in this area (suffering, death)…in honest dialogue, the educator should not put down any position, but motivate all participants to think further. Like Job, children are able to ask questions. (Korneck in Lawson 2012, p.431)

Islam

Islam is a religion, a civilisation and a way of life, having its roots in a reformation of Judaism and Christianity which had become distorted by pagan influences. Mohammed, born in Mecca (570–632 CE), was given a message to learn and repeat to others, now collected in the Qur'an (the Recitation). Knowledge of Islam comes mainly from the Qur'an which is divided into 114 suras each of which begins 'In the name of God, the Lord of Mercy, the Giver of mercy.'

This world is transitory; Muslims accept it because it is what they experience. Life is a journey to find the meaning of existence and contentment. Mohammed found this through the message that was revealed to him: belief in one God, prayer, fasting, pilgrimage, giving to the poor could lead to a transformed life. Humans are free to choose to follow God's way and accept a life which is God's gift. Death is not to be feared for it is a meeting with God who desires to call back God's creation to himself. The time, place or type of death is not known. Life after death, resurrection, is an act of faith, the Qur'an states 'Who will give life to bones while they are disintegrating? ... He will give them life who produced them the first time; and He is, of all creation, Knowing' (Qur'an 36.78–80). At death there is a judging by a merciful God for the Muslim to give an account of his life. The judging is a response to God's attributes of justice and mercy, which have no meaning if there is no life after death. For those who have followed God's way, there is a garden of paradise; for those who have failed, the fires of hell. Children are not judged by the Qur'an's rules, since they are learning, so if death intervenes they go straight to Paradise.

The Qur'an states that each child is born free from any sin or blemish. The newborn is born in a natural state *fitvah* which is inclined towards good. The idea of inherited sin is not found in Islam. There are three developmental stages in childhood: the first seven years are for play and exploration, the child is encouraged to discover creation; the second seven years are those of discipline and learning, the child learns the consequence of actions and human interrelationships; at fourteen following the introduction to the tenets and beliefs of Islam, the Qur'an states that the young person is accountable for his or her actions (Syeed and Ritchie, p.298). The above suggests that, while grieving is done for a child who dies, the devout parents can know that they will meet their dead child again in Paradise.

Hinduism

Hinduism is flexible; it is more like a family of religions:

> It is difficult...to say who a Hindu is. To be a Hindu, a person may observe a complicated system of rules – or none at all. One may give up the world, or accept it; one may worship one god, or many gods. One may worship a man as a god, as many do in India, or one may worship no god at all, and yet be a Hindu. (Brown 1975, p.63)

Yet central to the different expressions of the religion is the doctrine of Karma since karma is the belief that whether or not the atman (soul) returns to this life, in a higher or lower animal/human form, or ceases to be born and becomes one with Reality, depends on the actions of the individual Hindu. However there is hope in that Hinduism's sacred book the *Gita* says, 'whenever there is an imbalance between the power of good and the power of evil, then I, Krishna, appear in a form to balance them up, to cut down the evil and increase the good' (Brown 1975, p.251).

Buddhism

Buddhism is challenging; it differs from other religions since it has no God, nor Saviour, it puts salvation completely within the grasp of a human. Siddhartha, his own name, and Gautama, the family name (563–477 BCE), lived a life of luxury in Bihar, destined to follow his father as king. But outside the palace he discovered old age, disease and death as unavoidable sufferings for all humans; he also saw a hermit, tranquil and serene and decided to be like him. These challenging, existential encounters led Siddhartha to leave and seek liberation from suffering by leading the life of an ascetic. After years of fasting, almost to death, and facing temptation to give up he sat under a Bodhi tree. One night an answer came, and from then he was called the Buddha – the Enlightened One. He taught for over forty five years, dying in his eighties.

The Buddha taught the Four Noble Truths: to recognise life as suffering, disease and death; to see the origin of suffering as a craving for impermanent achievement and possessions; to cease attachments, finding liberation from these in joy, happiness and peace – Nirvana; to follow the path that leads to cessation between self-indulgence and asceticism: the noble eight fold path of right view, right thinking, right speech, right action, right livelihood, right diligence, right mindfulness and right concentration which leads to peace. A man must trust himself and summon the powers within him to achieve his goals in life: 'be ye refuges unto yourselves; be your own salvation with earnestness and high results, work out you salvation with diligence' (Brown 1975, p.129).

The law of Karma, or action, is created with the body, speech or mind and leaves a subtle imprint on our mind which has the potential to bring future happiness or future suffering, depending on whether our actions bring happiness or suffering to others; the positive brings life; the negative death. A person is born and reborn, that which is successively reborn is not a continuing entity, 'the karma-bearing "subtle body", but the stream of karma itself' (Hick 1989, p.491) since there is no belief in a soul. Parallels are drawn with the caterpillar and the butterfly – they are the same but not the same. The goal is Nirvana which literally means 'dying out'. Nirvana is called 'the harbour of the refuge', 'the cool cave', 'the island among the floods'. The end of suffering', 'the calm of existence' will continue as long as there is a desire for existence (Brown 1975, p.131).

Drawing together experience and cultural context leading to practical implications

There are several events which potentially result in difficult grieving for children. These include the loss of an expected sibling through a mother's miscarriage or a stillbirth; the terminal illness of a close relative, particularly that of a parent and sometimes a close grandparent who has been significant in the life of the child; the terminal illness of the child and the effect on child siblings; the loss of a child through an accident and the grief of a sibling; the suicide of someone close including a child or adolescent. Young children are very resilient. They pick up the sadness emerging on these occasions from the adults in their lives, though if they are protected and not told in suitable language what has happened they may feel guilt and think that they are in some way responsible for the death. Informing children using language appropriate to them is tough but necessary. Resources to help adults sustain bereaved children are varied. Many adult hospices have a bereavement department with trained volunteers who are able to work with the children of the patients. Sixty per cent of adults die in hospitals where bereavement counselling for the children of patients is limited in the UK, due to government cuts to the NHS. However, chaplains are able to help. Another source of help is the Childhood Bereavement Network whose website (see Useful Websites and Organisations) provides a geographical directory of available support services. It is campaigning for better provision with the slogan 'Grief matters for children'. In June 2007, the UK government set up the Bereavement Advice Centre offering a freephone helpline and a range of literature. A useful download from its website is *My Grandad Plants People!* (Earl n.d.), a simple guide for adults when children ask questions about death.

ACTIVITIES TO ELICIT THE READER'S EXPERIENCE

1. Think of an experience you have had in which a death was difficult to handle. Write down what you did to help and what you could have done with the knowledge gained from this chapter.

2. Look up one of the websites mentioned and assess its use to you.

4

What Should We Tell Children and Adolescents?

What scares me is the forever part. I wish they would make life longer and Heaven shorter.
(Julia in Marshall 2003, p.29)

I like the idea of heaven but I'm not in any hurry to get there.
(Paul in Marshall 2003, p.85)

A child's experience

Jim's grandad died just before Christmas. Jim was six. His grandad had owned a bakery in a village, and people would queue to buy fresh bread every morning. He had also made wonderful cakes, especially special cakes for birthdays and weddings. Jim was matter of fact when he was told of his grandad's death, since it was near Christmas, and he said that grandad would be able to cook Jesus a birthday cake.

Reflection on experience

Children can be very matter of fact when told of a death. Jim came from a home where Christian festivals had meaning. He associated Jesus' birth and childhood with his own experience of birthdays, which included celebrating by having a special birthday cake made by Grandad. The timing of his granddad's death coincided with preparations for Christmas, so Grandad would be busy making a cake to celebrate Jesus' birthday. Jim's understanding of heaven was a continuation of life as he experienced it here, grandad making cakes.

An adolescent's experience

Jenny was twelve when her mother died of cancer at the family home. Her mother had been looked after by her own mother. Whenever Jenny asked her grandmother about her mother's health, she was told that her mother was getting better. One day she returned home from school to find her mother and her grandmother gone. The bedroom was empty. Jenny later discovered that her mother had died and her body had been taken to the funeral directors.

Reflection on experience

Although Jenny was shocked when she saw her mother's empty bed, she had already begun to anticipate her mother's death through noticing changes in her mother. She was getting weaker, sleeping more and having increasing doses of painkillers, including a syringe driver. Young people need to be told the truth, even if it is hard to take and has difficult life-changing repercussions. Adolescents observe the situation and are wise enough to know what is actually happening. Being deceived by an adult family member sows the seed of a lack of trust in other adults.

It may well be that Grandma was in denial of her daughter dying. However, it could not have been easy for Jenny's grandmother to think about the possibility of her own daughter's dying and death: a young person who had a future and children to bring up. It is never easy when a person is predeceased by their own offspring. She was also of an age and generation that did not talk about death.

As adults we need to listen to children and adolescents. This listening will give us clues to our approach and what to tell them to help them understand the situation of a terminally ill parent and to reassure them that life will go on despite a death. They can be helped to see that they will be able to carry the lost parent, and memories of their parenting, with them throughout their future lives, as part of their own life story.

Linking adult, child and adolescent experience

How do we tell children that someone close to them is terminally ill? How could a family member have prepared Jenny and her younger sisters for their mother's death? This chapter will look in detail at the relationship between the child or adolescent and an adult, who may be a parent, teacher or nurse, in preparing the youngsters for the death of a terminally ill mother, telling them about dying, helping them at the death, and being available to be alongside the child or adolescent after the death.

Many parents still shelter their children from death, for example by replacing a dead pet in the hope that a child will not notice and will not have to be told about death nor the parent answer difficult questions. This can also be done by not allowing children to attend the funeral of a grandparent, teacher or school mate. Parents fill every moment of life, ignoring mortality, turning off media reports of war and famine in far-off places, until the truth is brought home when the troops return in coffins. Yet children cannot be protected from death since they are aware of it from an early age, when they see a dead bird which has fallen from a nest, a squashed hedgehog on the road or their pet is discovered to be cold and still, as was Alex's guinea pig in Chapter 2.

Adults do not respond to young children's questions about death, yet children experience death and accept it without question. Examples are noted in Chapter 3, such as the experience of Patricia's body lying at home on the settee with her younger siblings playing around her and the cat curled up on her feet. In a BBC Radio broadcast (Woman's Hour, Radio 4, 5 December 2015) a mother spoke of keeping the body of her dead child at home and the siblings playing naturally in the dead child's bedroom, stroking his hair and kissing him.

It is not morbid to talk to children about death; it is their right to be helped to understand and be informed if they ask questions. As adults in a western society, we are reluctant to talk about dying and death, and we have certain ideas about children, believing that they have an innocence of suffering and mortality which must be preserved from such dark subjects, but an understanding of death is part of a child's 'primary socialisation', which is crucial for a basic childhood psychological grasp and interpretation of reality. Yet today many parents are reluctant themselves to visit a deceased parent in the Chapel of Rest and do not think it suitable for children to visit, neither do they allow children to attend a funeral (see Chapter 6). Therefore children and adolescents do not learn how to grieve through observation, since family members attempt to hide their grief lest the children see adults crying. We do not want to expose children to the fact of death if, as adults, we can avoid it.

Sociological, psychological and historical insights

Whether you are a parent, or one of the professionals involved in bereavement care, you need to bear in mind a number of things if you are to tell children and adolescents difficult news and respond to their subsequent questions. 'Telling' is a tough journey, though a necessary one. A parent may opt out of telling her children, hoping that someone else will do it, but if no one does a child may feel isolated from others, abandoned and deserted. Adults don't like to talk about death, especially if it is of a young parent who shouldn't be dying and who is needed by her children, nor is it right for a child to lose a parent. Ana Draper in her booklet *Good Grief: What Will We Tell the Kids?* notes that:

> studies show that good communication really helps the grieving process – and a good process before someone dies can really help a child to re-establish their life and to re-imagine their future without their loved one – one without their loved one, yes, but a positive nevertheless, in which the memory of, and connection with the person they've lost helps them to live their own lives as fully as they can. (Draper 2008, p.2)

Time spent preparing when faced with this difficult task of telling youngsters that Mum is dying is valuable. It is important to build up trust with the child since the process of bearing bad news is a continuing task; children will have further questions and anxieties as the illness progresses, creating a need for ongoing information.

A parent telling a child

Using the example of a mother dying, the father has his own grief to face when he hears of a terminal diagnosis. He has to come to terms with an emotional whirlwind. One husband whose wife, a nurse, in a routine examination found a sinister shadow on her pancreas said:

> From that moment there was never a morning that I did not wake without a sense of dread, not unlike fear, buried the gnawing hole I felt in my gut… I would gladly and gratefully have given anything for it to be me and not her. (Oliver 2013, p.1)

and later:

> Watching the one you love most go through so much, and over a relatively long and intense time, is profoundly traumatic, and is probably made worse by the fact that much has to be suppressed simply in order to cope with what is happening day by day. (Oliver 2013, p.7)

A parent who has a relationship with a child from birth knows the personality of that child and can talk honestly and appropriately. She is the closest resource to the child. However, a parent needs to be aware and accepting of her own mortality since a child, when told of her mother's illness, may suddenly feel scared, or angry, or have the thought and ask the question, 'Will you die?' For a young parent who has not thought of her own mortality this may itself be a frightening and daunting question, but it needs to be answered and the child reassured that the parent is healthy and has a long, healthy life to share with the child, but, 'Yes, I will die at some stage in the distant future, since all living things die.' The information may need to be repeated since it may be a shock and may take the child time to assimilate.

When to start telling a child or adolescent?

Starting to talk is difficult; there is no good time to begin to tell a child bad news. There is no blueprint which indicates the relationship between age and understanding, how much the child wants to know or if the child would rather not know anything. Conversation with a young child is difficult since her attention span is limited, and, particularly with the emotions stirred by the news, she will jump from one thing to another, in and out of grief. The amount of information that a child can handle at any one time is limited; when that is reached a child may 'turn off' and substitute feelings they can handle for those they cannot. Give information a bit at a time – like pieces of a jigsaw which eventually build into a picture, or sections of an orange which you cannot eat all at once. The information can be put together by the child when needed.

What to tell a child if the cause of the illness is cancer

Winston's Wish has a useful resource: a book called *The Secret C: Straight talking about Cancer* (Stokes 2009). It is aimed at supporting parents or carers with the task of telling children and encourages open communication and questions about cancer through pictures, captions and straightforward language, while stressing the need to keep routines and still try to have some fun. It is aimed at children aged seven to ten.

A suggested way of approaching things is to ask the child what she has noticed about Mum. 'Have you noticed that Mum gets tired quicker or sits down more? Or begins to doze in the middle of a conversation?' Through these types of questions the father can discover where the child is in understanding the situation. It also gives the child some control of the conversation. The challenge of telling a child about a death and responding to questions about death is talking in a way a child will understand through knowing the stages of concept development. A baby up to about two has little language; what the baby has noticed is that the prime provider of security and love is missing and the baby feels unsafe. The mother is no longer available in the usual way, for example she may no longer be able to pick the baby up. A young child of two to five years realises that the 'mum that was' is not coming back so the child's security is threatened. The child needs a great sense of being cared for and comforted. A six- to twelve-year-old has become aware that everyone dies and may withdraw from family life and close adults in case they die. An adolescent is fully aware of mortality and may become detached, show anger or withdraw into a private world of her own. It is important when alongside a child or adolescent to recognise that each child moves at her own pace and grieves in her own way. Try not to be surprised, shocked or angered by what a child might say.

It is important to allow silence between parent and child. Don't be afraid of silence, it allows time for the child to gather her thoughts and try to make sense of what she is feeling. Adolescents want the facts. They want truth and honesty in what a parent tells them; it is likely that they will then confide and talk with their peer group. During puberty an adolescent is forming her own identity and is more distant from a parent. However, an adolescent is more aware of mortality. Adolescents are able to think in abstract terms, and handle news of a terminally ill parent and subsequent bereavement in very different ways from children. They can anticipate when a person is ill and dying, as Jenny did, and grieve in their own ways, which may be silence, a grief which is just as real as that of loud outbursts. Yet adolescents are complex creatures, since at the onset of puberty they are beginning to move into the adult world and gradually become their own person as they separate from the family. A girl will, however, need a mother as a model of the female gender, though she may later rebel against her mother's model and create her own.

An interesting resource to help with 'what to tell' a child is an American website called 'Aha Parenting'. Parents write in to a consultant, Dr Laura Markham. A particular request is from Lisa, the mother of a twenty-six-month-old daughter (Aha Parenting n.d.). Lisa's father is in hospital. The granddaughter bonded instantly on meeting her grandfather but geographically lives a long distance away so communicates by webcam. The letter is headed 'Explaining death to children', a request from Lisa for help in telling her daughter when her grandfather dies. Dr Markham suggests saying:

> Grandpa is very sick. He is old and his body doesn't work so well anymore, so it was weaker and got a disease. That disease is slowly shutting his body down. He will get weaker but will still be able to hear us even when he is lying very still. Eventually, though, his body will shut down totally. When that happens we will bury his body in the ground.
>
> You will be able to see his body and you will see that it doesn't really look much like him because his wonderful loving, laughing spirit is not there. We honor the body that is left, but it is more like

a home where Grandfather lived, more like a shell he has cast off because he no longer needs it.

As the illness progresses, so the situation changes for the family. Gradually the 'well' parent or partner may get more involved in the caring. This is an opportunity for the carer parent to ask the child why they think this is happening and how everyone in the family could make life more positive for Mum. Draper comments:

> An illness can challenge any beliefs about the future in an instant. This makes a child feel as if they have lost all control over their circumstances. You can help them to deal with this lack of control by talking about how you can all begin to take control of your new circumstances more effectively. (Draper 2008, p.7)

The children and adolescents in a family might come up with ideas like having a rota of household chores or each in turn spending time with Mum reading her a story. If Dad becomes the main carer, it could mean giving up his job and the family living with less money.

Telling of the death

The father's grief at his wife's eventual death is expressed by Oliver at the death of his wife:

> The convulsive, body-racking, uncontrollable flood. Anguish and lament. Sorrow and soundless scream. Protest and passion…I was exhausted, and I had to remind myself that I was not the only one grieving for (her). There was a growing torpor, and a heaviness like wading through deep water. (Oliver 2013, p.3)

It may therefore be difficult for a father to tell his children about their mother's death, nevertheless it is significant that outward grief is shared by both father and young. Child Bereavement UK states, 'seeing adults expressing emotion can give a child of any age "permission" to do the same if they feel they want to. Hearing how you are feeling may help them to consider their own feelings' (Schools Information Pack: Supporting Parents and Carers; see their website for details). Dr Markham suggests:

> We are all very sad because we love him so much and when his body shuts down we will never be able to hug him again. That's why we cry so much. It helps us to cry, just like it helps you to cry when you

fall down and get hurt. You cry and then you feel better. Because this is such a big hurt, we do a lot of crying. If you see me crying it is ok, it is because I am sad and miss my dad.

For a child the strong emotions around a bereavement may overwhelm. It may be the first time that a child has experienced the death of a close person, and it will take time for her to make sense and meaning of it in relation to her existing knowledge.

Draper believes that emotions are neither good nor bad:

> It is what you do with them that matters. The parent talking about his emotions can really help his child to understand what is happening. It is easy to withdraw from a child rather than show emotion. But that can make things harder because it seems like a punishment. Families tend to hide their emotions to protect children, which can lead a child and the family, to feel isolated. It is OK to express emotions... (Draper 2008, p.7)

Emotions in children are volatile. 'How could you leave me?' anger is followed by guilt that the child could even think such thoughts; children can use the feeling of self-pity to manipulate adults. There can be depression and the dead parent can become idealised. Boys in a family can be very violent in their grief, reacting to a death through fighting each other and trying to make each other cry, climbing and falling from trees, ending with scar-covered knees. Each emotion needs to be worked at as it is part of a journey: not to achieve closure but an ability to move on. Draper calls it 're-imaging', taking the deceased with the child in their memories of Mum.

The journey of loss continues into a journey of life. Ana Draper writes that 'Grief is all about constructing a lasting story that enables the living to integrate the memory of the dead person into their ongoing lives'(Draper 2008, p.17). Freud expressed it that, 'We will never find a substitute (after loss) and actually, this is how it should be, it is the only way of perpetuating that love which we do not want to relinquish.' Dr Markham states that for the toddler, Lisa might say, 'Grandpa would want us to keep living and enjoying life. We have to live extra full and good lives because we are living not just for ourselves now, but also for Grandfather, since he is in our hearts.' The advice given in the response of Dr Markham emphasised creating and reinforcing memories and sharing adult and child emotions over a death.

Resources to help when a parent dies

The Gingerbread website for single parents provides practical advice (see the Useful Websites and Organisations section). The bereavement charity Winston's Wish has a book called *A Child's Grief* (Stokes 2005), which helps any adult supporting a child through bereavement and death, offering practical suggestions and ideas. Another book produced by Winton's Wish is *Milly's Bugnut* (Janney 2002). Milly knows that when people die they can't come back, not in the way we want them, but this doesn't stop Milly wishing a secret and very important wish. She finds an unexpected answer to her heart's desire. The story was written by Jill Janney following the death of her children's father. *'It's OK to be Sad': Activities to Help Children Aged 4–9 Manage Loss, Grief and Bereavement* (Collins and Drakeford 2005) and *Supporting Young People Coping with Grief, Loss and Death* (Weymont and Rae 2006) are also helpful for both parents and professionals. A useful novel written by Max Porter, *Grief is the Thing with Feathers* (2015), has emerged from the writer's experience of the loss of his own father when he was a young child. The novel explores the lives of a man and his two young sons at the sudden death, in a fatal accident, of his wife and their mother. The man tries to cope on his own with great difficulty and the progress of his loss is followed and helped by a crow. The main character is a Ted Hughes scholar and the bird is an image taken from the late poet and writer Ted Hughes. The crow stays with the family, saying of himself, 'Perfect device doctors, ghosts and crows. We can do things other characters can't, like eat sorrow, un-birth secrets and have theatrical battles with language and God' (Porter 2015, p.15).

Dr Markham has an interesting section in her response to Lisa about her toddler, she writes:

> It is possible that your daughter will remain very connected to her grandfather. There are many accounts of people who remember when a grandparent died during their childhoods, who say that they continued to speak with, and even see, their loved one. The younger the person is, the more likely they are to actually see the loved one after the death, because there is no cultural overlay to tell them it's not possible. Some people may say this is real. Some people may say it is a defense against the finality of death. I believe it does not matter, since it is a very adaptive response that has only healthy effects on

the child. But even if she does not see him, it will help her if you encourage her to speak with him inside her own head. If she can have a small object of his to keep and hold, it will facilitate this. Kids who are able to maintain a relationship with the person they've lost, even as they have permission to go on living fully and joyfully, make the healthiest adjustment to loss.

Research is sparse, particularly among children, on questions of contact with the deceased. Many religious circles believe it to be wrong. Their reasoning is based on references in the Old Testament such as Deuteronomy 18.11: 'No one shall be found among you…who seeks oracles from the dead.' Humanists, agnostics and atheists are critical, asserting that these experiences are 'grief-induced hallucinations' based on wish-fulfilment, imagination, magical thinking, fantasy, memories and emotional needs. An organisation called After-Death Communication Experiences (ADCs) researched 2000 North Americans aged 8–92 years from diverse cultural backgrounds, collecting over 3300 accounts from people who believe that they have been contacted by a deceased relative or friend (1995–2016). They estimated that at least 60 million Americans, 20 per cent of the population of the USA, had such an experience. The result was an incredible sense of peace providing comfort, hope and profound emotional and spiritual healing. Dr Markham suggested that the younger the person was, the more likely it was that she could communicate that she 'saw' a deceased person. A *Scientific American* article notes that bereavement is a time 'when hallucinations are particularly common…the presence of the deceased is the norm rather than the exception' people 'find them comforting as if they are re-connecting with something of the positive from the person's life' (Bell 2008). A website Perceptive Children Support Forum receives parents' questions. One of the children for whom advice was sought was two years old. The response from Athena Drewes, a licensed child psychologist, parapsychologist and consultant to the Rhine Research Center at Duke University and the Parapsychology Foundation of Children's psychic experiences, can be read on the website (Drewes n.d.).

The use of euphemisms
Adults sometimes avoid the word 'death' by using euphemisms when talking to children. The Oxford English Dictionary defines a

euphemism as 'a mild or less direct word used rather than one that is blunt or may be considered offensive'. The word is derived from Greek meaning, 'to speak well' or 'good talk'. The word was used as a euphemism by the ancient Greeks meaning, 'to keep a holy silence', that is 'to speak well by not speaking at all'. Underlying the word is an attempt to disguise and refuse to take responsibility for a truth since, as adults, we want to escape thoughts of our finitude and mortality.

A real problem with euphemisms is that young children are concrete, literal thinkers and so understand words at their face value. The statement, 'Grandma's gone to be with Jesus' may get the response, 'I love Grandma. Can I go with her?' Cranwell (2007) reports an incident when 'Pat aged ten, remembered that at an early age she was told that her great-grandmother had "gone away". After a few weeks, she asked: "When is she coming back?" The response was: "sorry, I forgot to tell you – she died."' He continued:

> Five years after the event, she summed up her feelings: 'If somebody said to me now: "She's gone away," it would be like telling a lie. It's best if you say, "She's died". Then you'd cry, and then it's over with.' It is to be noted that the hindsight is that of an adolescent whose understandings of death are different from that of a child. (Cranwell 2007, pp.20–21)

The statement on the death of a favourite granddad, 'Grandad's gone on a journey' or 'gone on a holiday', or 'gone to a better place', may each receive the child's response, 'When is he coming back?' or 'Where's he gone. Can I go?' Similarly in response to the statement, 'We've lost Joe', a child may ask, 'Where did he get lost?' In newspaper 'death notices' similar euphemisms are used. Does it mean that adults cannot face talking about death? The euphemisms we use can have detrimental effects on children, who may become angry about the death or feel guilty that they are somehow responsible for the person 'going away'. The statement that a loved one has 'gone to sleep' may lead a child to be fearful of going to bed. A friend told me that when her mother died, her nephew who was on holiday with her, looked into the sky and said, 'that star shining brightly is Gran.' Another child looked up into the starry sky and asked, 'Which one is Granny?' Euphemisms may be suitable for very small children who will not have the concepts of death and finality, but as the child gets older, this will change and evolve, as children are able to understand concrete language.

On occasions, in religious families, comments can be made to children such as, 'Jesus wanted her for an angel', or 'God took him'. One lad, whom a colleague worked with and whose parents were Christians, said that God had taken his grandfather and he was now in heaven. Bob was very angry with God, for he wanted his grandfather to play football. God wasn't fair taking grandfather. The colleague was not religious yet knew that she needed to honour the family's beliefs but was not sure how to tackle the anger. Eventually, she helped Bob to see that it was the cancer that took his grandfather and not God.

The death and family members

At a death, other family members who would normally help to protect and support the child may be caught up in their own grief. It seems only natural, in this context, for a parent to try to protect a child from her own grief. The trouble is that when everyone becomes too afraid to speak about how they are feeling, or about the person who has died, it is unhelpful. The silence that follows can stall the entire process by which collective grief can help a new, positive story to emerge.

When a parent dies, the surviving parent may become dependent on the child or children, for instance the older child becoming 'a little mum', but this must be avoided; a child or adolescent needs to be just that, having time with friends her own age, not swallowed up in adult roles. This will need the help of other family members. It is likely that the surviving parent may be too wrapped up in her own grief to talk to the children, then family members, neighbours close to the family or professionals may help. Being there is a comfort and reassurance to children.

Involvement of others in the support of children – school

A child living with a parent with a terminal illness will value the regularity and stability of school, the ordinariness of it. Yet a parent needs to tell the school of an impending death in a family. News of the terminal illness of a mother will affect a child and this will be carried into everyday life in school.

It is important for the parent to inform the school of the death of his wife. The school should liaise with the family, where possible, and establish what the child knows since young children may fantasise to gain attention, while conflicting information from home and school confuses the child, who then loses trust in the adults. At a convenient stage, agreement needs to be reached as to what information is to be given, and to whom, before the pupil returns to school. On the death of a child's parent, permission should be asked from the child before telling the school. Conversations between school and family, including the bereaved child, will determine how the news should be given to the school community, the child's class or whole school in a primary school and the tutor group in a secondary school.

A bereaved child may be encouraged by her family to go back to school soon after the death, since it is a routine and the agenda of school work is life rather than death. School may be particularly significant to a child with friendship groups. School may well be a refuge for a child from the emotions and the ongoing grief of family at home, bringing a sense of normality to life.

Believers' experiences – world faiths

Judaism

In the Hebrew scriptures, Jacob was travelling across the trade route home to his own country to meet and be reconciled with his twin brother, Esau, whom he had wronged many years before. He travelled with wives, children, slaves and animals. His feelings and emotions must have been jangled, one minute wanting to rush ahead and get the meeting over, the next wanting to hold back from a difficult encounter. This went on until he recognised that neither his flocks with their young, nor his children could be rushed; he had to go at 'the pace of children' (Genesis 33.4–15). Today adults need to learn this lesson. We need to recognise the conceptual development of children/ adolescents, so that what we tell them is age related and be guided by their pace.

For Jews in biblical times, education began early. As soon as children could speak, they learnt by heart the first phrase of the Shema 'hear Israel, the Lord is our God the Lord is one…' (Deuteronomy 46.4–9), which ends with the words of the commandments, 'to love the Lord your God with all your heart and with all your soul and with all your might and you shall teach them (the commandments) diligently to your children'. To 'teach them' means 'impress upon them'. The

Shema represented the central affirmation of the Jewish faith and was recited morning and evening by adults (Deuteronomy 6.4–5). Children were to be taken seriously: their purpose was as learners of the Torah (Deuteronomy 6.6–9, 11.13–21; Numbers 15.37–41). Within the legislation all, including children, were called every seventh year to the public reading of the Torah (Deuteronomy 31.10–13). As soon as he can speak, his father teaches a boy the Shema, Torah and the sacred tongue; otherwise, it were better he had not come into the world (Tosefta Hagigah 1, 2).

Children learnt by being alongside parents in the fields. There was a rhythm of work and leisure: the weekly Sabbath and the annual cycle of the major festivals, associated with agriculture (cf. Exodus 23.14–17; Deuteronomy 11.13–15, 16.1–7; Leviticus 23.4–44). The Passover festival marked the beginning of the barley harvest and recalled the Exodus. Pentecost followed, marking the wheat harvest and the giving of the Torah on Mount Sinai. The feast of Tabernacles at the end of September celebrated the end of the grape harvest and retold the wilderness wanderings. The festivals were celebrated and explained in the home, with children taking a leading role (Deuteronomy 6.2–22; Exodus 12.26f). The seder (Passover meal) required the meal to begin with a child asking questions about the purpose of the meal and the ritual. It ended with a child bargaining for the return of the afikoman (hidden matzoh bread) in Passover. There were four types of children: wise, wicked, simple and those who do not know how to ask. Each child has to be answered according to his own question and in line with his own attitude...these...encompass all of the combinations of learning and moral religious identity. At Passover, the major Jewish festival of national and personal liberation, four types of children are used to symbolize how all Israel struggles with growing in wisdom and goodness (Yust *et al.* 2006, p.51).

Josephus claimed that the Jewish tradition was distinguished by the care taken to instruct children. His claim is made within the context of emphasis on the special character of a lifestyle and commitment to preserve inherited Jewish piety as 'the most important duty in life.' Philo (25 BCE to 50 CE) claimed Jews had been trained 'from a very early age', even 'from the cradle to honour the One God alone and to observe the Jewish law'. Before the destruction of the temple (70 CE) there were 480 synagogues in Jerusalem, each of which had a Bible school. Schools supplemented the teaching of the parents in the home.

They were not a replacement for the home. The second-century rabbi Judah ben Tema said that children should be taught Scriptures at five years, the Mishnah at ten years, to fulfil the law at 13, and the Talmud at 15 years.

There was no education adapted for children. Children memorised sections of the book of Deuteronomy, becoming a people of the book. The degree of literacy cannot be determined. It is likely that learning was still a prerogative of the wealthy and largely that of male children. It is questionable whether children were of intrinsic worth for any innate qualities of character. It was through their preoccupation with learning and practising the Torah that children became significant. Rabbi Juda Nesiah stated 'the world stands only upon the breath of the schoolchildren' (210 CE).

Christianity

For suffering like that of Jenny's mum, Jenny's question is, 'Where is God in letting my mum die?' For those who have no faith the answer is that death is simply the natural end of a life. However, for Jenny's mum it was a life cut short by suffering. For a believer there are two questions. If God is love and in control, omnipotent, why do awful things like terminal illness happen? Second, is there a life beyond death, which gives hope and courage and might sustain through pain and suffering? Does suffering occur because this world is contrary to God's will or because God made it this way but intended it to be otherwise?

The dominant model of a Theology of Creation from the fourth to the eighteenth centuries was that: God created ex nihilo signifying that matter is good; Creation is finite and closed – everything has its God-given place, a closed system of cause and effect, a stable home for humans to prepare for eternity. Creation has a purpose. Humans are free agents who can choose or reject a relationship with God; at the end, suffering is justified in the overall plan of God. Irenaeus, the second-century bishop of Lyons, questioned this model. He taught that creation is emergent and purposeful, moving from innocence and immaturity to knowledge and complexity towards an end, the eschaton, when suffering is transformed in a new creation (Revelation 21.1–4).

Anthropologists state that the first humans struggled with a hostile environment, necessitating selfishness and violence to survive, but gradually became capable of the moral awareness of love and sacrifice, putting the need of others before personal needs. When God is not self-evident, there is a distance between humans and God, so that humans have freedom in relation to God. God is the world's foundation: not intervening but able to influence it through God's presence within human hearts. Hauerwas considers that: 'historically speaking, Christians have not had a "solution" to…suffering. Rather they have had a community of care that made is possible for them to absorb the destructive terror of evil that constantly threatens to destroy all human relations' (1990, p.53). Much suffering has no sense, but some sufferers use it creatively to grow, to develop fortitude and perseverance. For others their suffering challenges their faith in God, which may be lost.

If God loves, then this must include God's ability to suffer, for it is when I love that I can suffer for the loved one. When the mode of God's power is vulnerability, God is willing to be pushed to the margins becoming good news to suffering. In the cross the Son suffers God-forsakenness, the experience of many sufferers. It might be thought that this is in bearing the world's sin and rejection of him. Jesus said, 'I am the Resurrection and the Life', and often spoke according to the Gospels of the 'third day'; certainly the Resurrection of Jesus was central to the kerugma of the Early Church. Whatever happened on that first Easter day is a mystery.

As Christians we have hope and that hope is in a loving God. Nothing lies beyond the compassionate love of God. Paul encapsulated this in Romans 8.38–9 when he wrote:

> For I am convinced that neither death, nor life, nor angels, nor rulers, nor things present, nor things to come, nor powers, nor height, nor depth, nor anything else in all creation will be able to separate us from the love of God in Christ Jesus our Lord.

Islam

The Islamic scholar Said Nursi believes it is necessary to expose children early to belief in God and spirituality. 'The more children are exposed to a community observing religion and the easier it will be for them to understand religion and spirituality later in life' (Nursi 2002).

This is not necessarily done through teaching children, but through them watching their parents and the community observe and practice their faith. Yet children's faith is tested in the everyday of Western society. However, an example was set in the life of Mohammed, who was tested by the death of his father before he was born and his mother when he was only six, leaving him an orphan. Mohammed knew grief as a child himself through losing his parents, and as a father grieving the death of two sons as infants. He was sorely tested through experiences of death and children. The story of Mohammad's life is told to children and may well bring comfort in their situations of grief and bereavement.

Hinduism

Hinduism is so diverse that it is difficult to say what is particular to children. The stories found in the scriptures of Krishna and the different gods are told to children and may well help and inspire them to live lives helping others.

Buddhism

There are no teachings specifically for children, yet at the heart of Buddhism is the Buddha's Discourse on Loving Kindness: 'Cherish in your heart's boundless good will to all that lives' (Brown 1975, p.150). Buddhists send out thoughts of love and compassion, arising out of their own hearts, to family, friends, enemies, animals and to worlds beyond, giving strength to live the eight fold path that leads to the end of suffering and coming of Nirvana, joy. This is a 'feature' of Vesak, the name of the lunar month that falls in May, with the full moon day in that month called Vesak day. This sacred festival day has threefold significance: it is said that it is the day Buddha was born, attained enlightenment and died.

Drawing together experience and cultural context leading to practical implications

What children are told in regard to death depends on their age, level of maturity, their parents, their faith background, if any, and the culture in which the child is raised. Cultures differ; for example, in Papua New Guinea, the deceased's body is ceremonially laid in a boat, a lit candle inside and the vessel launched out into the water. This is a very visual ritual, suggesting the image of death as the last journey, and one into light.

We live in a global village where children, through the media, discover and hear about varying attitudes and customs connected with death and bereavement. Many of us live in multicultural areas where practices vary in the information given to children. Difference should be respected, yet children also need respect and to be encouraged to openly question and explore, particularly when they are faced with the terminal illness and death of a parent. A child can live through most things as long as adults talk to her and tell her the truth.

ACTIVITIES TO ELICIT THE READER'S EXPERIENCE

1. Use the account of the letter published on the 'Aha Parenting' website referred to in the text and given in full below. Read through the piece and comment on it, if possible in consultation with a parent who has a toddler of between two and two-and-a-half years.

Dear Lisa

...it is possible that your daughter will remain very connected to her grandfather. There are many accounts of people who remember when a grandparent died during their childhoods, who say that they continued to speak with, and even see, their loved one. The younger the person is, the more likely they are to actually see the loved one after the death, because there is no cultural overlay to tell them it's not possible. Some people may say this is real. Some people may say it is a defense against the finality of death. I believe it does not matter, since it is a very adaptive response that has only healthy effects on the child.

But even if she does not see him, it will help her if you encourage her to speak with him inside her own head.

The fact that your daughter bonded with your dad during his hospital stay suggests that they have a special relationship. The more connection they can have prior to his death, the better it will be for both of them.

As for what to say to her? Grandpa is very sick. He is old and his body doesn't work so well anymore, so it was weaker and got a disease. That disease is slowly shutting his body down. He will get weaker but will still be able to hear us even when he is lying very still. Eventually, though, his body will shut down totally. When that happens we will bury his body in the ground.

You will be able to see his body and you will see that it doesn't really look much like him because his wonderful loving, laughing spirit is not there. We honor the body that is left, but it is more like a home where Grandfather lived, more like a shell he has cast off because he no longer needs it.

Why is there death? That is one of the great mysteries of life. But look around at nature. Everything alive is born, grows up, has a full life, gets old and dies. It makes room for new life. Grandfather had a full life and one of the best parts was having his granddaughter to love.

When Grandfather's body goes, he will stay in our hearts. If we listen we will be able to feel him smiling at us and even speaking to us. One way to express our love is to tell stories about him and honor the life he led, so that is what we do at the funeral.

We are all very sad because we love him so much and when his body shuts down we will never be able to hug him again. That's why we cry so much. It helps us to cry, just like it helps you to cry when you fall down and get hurt. You cry and then you feel better. Because this is such a big hurt, we do a lot of crying. If you see me crying it is ok, it is because I am sad and miss my dad. You can always give me a hug, but you don't need to take care of me. I will be ok. Grandpa would want us to keep living and enjoying life. We have to live extra full and good lives because we are living not just for ourselves now, but also for Grandfather, since he is in our hearts.

There are also wonderful books to read to your daughter, which will help her (and probably you) to continue to process this major transition in your lives...

I wish you all blessings and the consolation of love.

Dr. Laura (Aha Parenting n.d.)

2.   Think about a child or adolescent with whom you work. How would you tell her about the impending death of a parent? Write your response as a dialogue.

5

Schools Coping with Bereavement and Death

If you believe in God, he'll take care of all the details.
(Winston in Marshall 2003, p.13)

A child's experience

A young child wanted to draw a card on Father's Day but was not allowed to by his teacher because she knew that his father had died. The boy said that it wasn't fair, 'I do have a father; I just can't see him' (Job and Francis 2004). Another child said about her first day at school that at the school gate she noticed all the mums, and 'there I was with Dad, because my mum has died'.

Reflection on experience

Some dates may be distressing to a bereaved child such as Father's Day or Mothering Sunday. Young children can feel left out if they have been bereaved. They want to be like their classmates, yet in some ways they are not. A child may feel sad and tearful at the death of a parent, or angry that the parent has 'deserted' and left him by dying. A child may be bullied in the playground for not being like other children, embarrassed or not sure how to react. For a young child, school is in some ways an extension of home in that there are adults who are the authority and dependable figures. Teachers need to know how best to support a bereaved child.

An adolescent's experience

An adolescent began unconsciously writing all her school work in mirror writing. The girl was disturbed about her involuntary squiggles. Her teacher recognised what was happening and took her aside. The teacher, with the use of a mirror, showed the girl that she was reversing the words. Later the teacher discovered that the girl was missing her mother who had died the previous year and was upset because she could no longer 'picture' her mum. The teacher asked if her mother had a sister and discovered a favourite aunt living nearby who had photos of her sister. She suggested that the girl asked her aunt if she could see the pictures. Being able to look at the photos and talk to her aunt helped the girl to remember and gradually in school her writing returned to normal.

Reflection on experience

Adolescents are finding their own feet and don't want to be 'exposed' in front of their peers. The teacher realised that something was upsetting the girl and took her aside on her own to see if she could help. The teacher had played about with mirror writing as a child and realised what the squiggles were. The sensitivity to her pupil's needs enabled her to come alongside the girl and help her.

Linking adult, child and adolescent experience

In the early part of the twentieth century, adults considered that death was not a 'subject' to be talked about with a child since children were innocent of such events, nor should it be mentioned in school since death was a private, family affair. It is now realised that young children may experience death and bereavement. From an early age, a young child is trying to make meaning from experience and integrating it with existing knowledge. Experiences of death are events that need such integration and could be introduced as part of their early life. The process of integration continues at home and at school.

In one nursery class, the home corner was decorated as a hospital with bottles of coloured sweets for pills, stethoscopes and nurses uniforms to encourage imaginative play. One three-year-old was sitting on a row of chairs very still. When asked by the teacher what she was doing, the child looked up in astonishment that the teacher did not know; 'I'm dead, of course' was the response. The teacher quickly took the child to another part of the room and a different activity rather than discover why she associated hospitals with death. The teacher did not attempt to explore with the child her thinking. What experience had led the three-year-old to associate hospitals with death rather than view them as places of healing, though sometimes recovery is not possible and a person becomes too ill and dies? Death for this teacher was 'swept under the carpet'. It may have been that the teacher did not know what to say (see Chapter 4) or did not know how to tackle the subject with such a young child (see concept development in children, Chapters 1 and 2).

Many adolescents are more 'worldly wise' about death and bereavement. Rosie, an only child, was 14 years old and preparing for her mock GCSEs when her mother died of cancer in the local hospice following a recurrent brain tumour. The death had been expected and Rosie and her father were present at her mother's death. She did not want her school told of her bereavement. However, she lived in a rural area and news travels fast so members of the school knew without being told by the family. Rosie chose to return to school several days after her mother's death. Rosie's behaviour is a route that adolescents and children may take in the face of death. School represents normality and a friendship group beyond the immediate emotional suffering of family, a peer group with whom to share confidences rather than the adults in her life. Adolescents are hormonal and have their own identity in process of formation. Rosie wanted to get on with her life. She also thought that getting on with her exam preparation was what her mother would have wanted.

Sociological, psychological and historical insights

Ninety-two per cent of children and young people will experience a 'significant' bereavement before the age of 16. Up to 70 per cent of schools have a bereaved pupil on their roll at any time. One in twenty-nine school-age children will have been bereaved of a parent or sibling; one in eighteen has been bereaved of a close friend (Child Bereavement UK 2009; see the Useful Websites and Organisations section).

The school community has a central role in being alongside pupils and staff in bereavement. Current research explores grief as a social construct, varying across communities. This involves considering proactive and reactive strategies associated with good outcomes for bereavement and loss. The social context of school is vital. Research demonstrates the significance of bereavement support from peers and trusted adults in the school community, in addition to that given by parents. This social support is enough for some children; for example, if, following a critical incident such as an accident involving a school bus, 'experts' come into school from outside, the bereavement process may be prolonged: the ongoing support from known, caring adults in school is more significant than that of outsiders. Children are resilient and may cope by simply knowing that each of them is valued, as an individual, and that help is readily available should they ask.

The significance of schools working with the family

Loss is part of our everyday lives, not separate from the ordinary life of home and school – pupils need an integrated approach within home and school, of pastoral care and their learning. A school is a social community and can offer a necessary routine to a child for whom home and family life following a significant death, such as that of a parent or loved grandparent, may have become emotionally charged and chaotic. School may even be an escape for a bereaved child or adolescent, since there are no reminders of a loss. If showing grief is the need of the pupil, school is a safe place since school personnel are diverse; for children there are the adults, teaching and support staff; for adolescents there is the peer group of friends and pastoral care staff. Together, these people represent a potentially broad range of help. The adults in school are not necessarily emotionally involved in the loss and, since they are outside the family, they can act as 'a listening ear', a confidant and a resource for a pupil. School staff can access specialist outside service providers, including counsellors, psychiatrists and social workers; these are a significant resource. A school library can include a section on bereavement and loss. There can be story books, factsheets and videos, and for adolescents in particular, access to telephone numbers of confidential 'helplines' which, with social media, are an important resource for adolescents in particular. A list of appropriate websites and phone numbers can be made available by a school on a piece of laminated card the size of a credit card ready to give to a needy adolescent. (See the Useful Websites and Organisations section.)

The approach to death in schools can be varied

Some schools' approach can be called 'crisis management', in that when a death occurs the school takes some reactive action. A second approach is when schools see anything to do with an actual death, or education about death and bereavement, as 'pathological' since death is still something of a taboo subject. A third approach is when schools see death as part of life and are prepared for it by a bereavement policy. These schools work in two ways: first, pastoral care, in other words how to work with and support the pupil, the family and the school community in bereavement; and second, sensitive teaching across the curriculum. Both pastoral care and the curriculum promote, cultivate and educate about healthy grief and ways to be supportive to a grieving pupil.

Creating a school policy for the pastoral care of bereaved pupils

A pupil may experience the death of a close family member, a fellow pupil or a favourite teacher and his grief may spill out into life in school. Having a policy in a school helps when a bereavement arises, particularly with sudden, multiple or traumatic circumstances. The Critical Incident Procedure is the prerogative of the head teacher. The policy needs to be a framework rather than prescriptive, agreed by school staff (teaching and non-teaching) and the governors; parent governors can be helpful as 'sounding boards'. The area of 'loss' is particularly emotive and therefore needs a policy statement which is sensitive enough to meet the needs of different situations of loss. It is likely that a policy may need to be formulated in the same format as other policies in the school so the information below is a suggestion only. It is important that the policy is regularly reviewed in the light of experience (see details in Appendix 1).

Examples of pastoral care in school
A school supporting a pupil with a life-limiting illness and their family

It is distressing for a teacher to discover that a pupil is suffering from an incurable illness. This will inevitably bring challenges to the classroom and the school, yet it is in sharing the individual's journey that the lives of those in contact with the pupil can be enriched. Many pupils with a life-threatening illness want to continue to attend school for as long as possible, since it gives a normality to life with an emphasis on living rather than dying, a continuation of friendships, and a sense of child or adolescent identity rather than that of patient identity. It is useful to have one person, staff or ancillary member of staff, as a regular contact with the family, so that all the school staff are aware of changes in the health and medical treatment of the child and can, if needed, change their methods of support. This also gives a message of support to the family.

If a pupil is receiving treatment at a local hospice or hospital, it may be possible for a nurse to come in and explain to the class how they can help. This will need the family's permission. At the point when the health of the child begins to deteriorate and attendance at school becomes more intermittent, or the child enters a children's hospice, his class can be invited to write and draw pictures to send to the child telling him what they are doing and keeping him in touch. When later the child dies, with family permission the class can be informed. It is important to decide who breaks the news to the class so that rumours do not abound and questions are answered by staff. At this point, how the school might respond needs to be thought through: if pupils can be represented at the funeral, whether the school might hold its own special assembly, and whether a lasting memorial is appropriate. The members of the class will grieve in their own ways.

The death of a member of staff

This is likely to affect the whole community in a primary school, since with the relatively small size of many such schools, particularly in a rural area, the deceased will be known by almost everyone. Helping pupils and staff will need great sensitivity, particularly if the death was sudden and unexpected. Contact with the family is helpful by phone or a visit so that their wishes may be honoured in the giving of information. It is helpful if this is done by an identified member of staff (see Appendix 2). It is important to give the information to a meeting of staff as soon as possible, ensuring that absent or part-time staff are also made aware. With the family's permission, the pupils need to be told in words that are clear and suitable to their developmental stage. This is best done in their class groups by a familiar teacher or the head teacher if the class teacher is young and may not have had experience of the death of someone close. The information may need to be repeated since it will be a shock to pupils and take the children time to assimilate the news. My youngest sister died of a brain tumour. She was a classroom assistant in a school for children with learning difficulties. When her death was announced, one boy refused to believe it saying, 'But she was my friend'.

The children may well ask questions which need to be answered. Feelings and emotions may be shown. The teacher should be willing to show her feelings as an adult: this helps children to realise that death is painful and final and it is appropriate to be sad. Children may want to talk and share their memories of the person, make a memory board, write a message or draw a picture to send to the bereaved family, or make cards of condolence for the family. This will help the bereaved to know that they are not alone and will be a positive way for children to express their emotions. Story books can be used to read to the children, which again helps them to explore death through the eyes of another person, for example *The Cooper Tree* (Robinson and Straky 2014), an illustrated book for young children on the death of their teacher.

The death of a pupil's parent

Some children in the class may need particular help in their grief. Informing the school is important for the parent. The family may decide to convey the message of the death by sending a letter to be read out in school; the bereaved child may or may not wish to be present when this happens. The school should liaise with the family, where possible, and establish what the child knows since young children may fantasise to gain attention, while conflicting information from home and school confuses the child, who then loses trust in the adults. Pupils need to be told – this is best done in their class groups. The teacher giving the news could be prepared to respond to any questions the children might have. There may be such questions as 'Where is she now?' (the deceased parent), which may be metaphysical about a life after death, an appropriate answer being that people believe different things about life after death. Others may ask a straightforward question about where the body is now. There may be questions about what happens now, including some about cremation and burial. It is important to help children understand that after death the body does not feel anything and does not need food or drink, so cannot be hurt or feel pain or fear.

The class teacher of the pupil whose parent has died needs to keep a record of significant dates – the date of death; the birthday; of Mothering Sunday or Father's Day – and be sensitive when the school breaks for Christmas, when there will be sadness with an empty chair at home. These will be significant occasions in the grieving process and will reoccur. This 'bereavement history of significant dates' should be in a child's file throughout the pupil's school life.

Pastoral care of a pupil returning to school

Returning to school may be frightening for a young child; he may think of death as contagious and therefore fear that while away from home someone else in the family might die. This may be a 'trigger time' which causes emotions to be freely expressed. Teachers need to read this sign and act appropriately when the time comes.

If a child acts differently from what is considered 'normal behaviour' a teacher could wonder, 'What does the child believe that is making him act differently?' If the belief can be addressed that will help. For example, sometime after her mother's death, Susie, Jenny's youngest sister, heard a friend of her mother's say at the school gate that if it hadn't been for the pregnancy with Susie, her mother would still be alive (see 'An adolescent's experience' at the beginning of Chapter 4). Susie came to believe that it was her fault that her mother had died. She became withdrawn and quiet. A teacher helped Susie to unpick this information, so that she could understand that actually pregnancy would have slowed a cancer that was already present in her mother's body and not caused it. With this knowledge, Susie regained her resilience.

The school is likely to need to cope with behaviour patterns that differ from the norm. Taking a bereaved child aside, a teacher can acknowledge what has happened. Allow crying if that is what the pupil needs; make sure that he has an 'escape' from class if he cannot cope; make allowances for loss of concentration or problems with school work; and be aware the child may experience bullying for 'being unusual', 'an oddity' and for not having a mother. The child may begin to bully others, to show that he has some authority and control of a situation. Teachers working with children in the context of a death can rely on their own humanity. The wisdom gained through their life experience underlies their work with bereaved children. A professional should trust themselves and their intuition, having built a level of trust with the child. A child needs to feel safe to trust and talk.

A major way of supporting a bereaved child or adolescent is to listen and encourage him to talk about his loss and express his feelings, whether anger or sadness, but always with a box of tissues handy. Listening is the key requirement at news of a death. Listen more than talk. Allow emotions, letting the child openly express feelings of anger, guilt and sadness. Tell the child that it is OK to show emotions; crying releases us and begins the process of healing. Professionals should not be shocked by the questions and need to say when they do not know the answer. Listen intently to children's strivings to make sense of a loss. Do not force children to talk but encourage and answer questions simply and honestly when they appear interested. A teacher might need to listen to a repeated story; even if it is the same story each time, give the pupil time. Say 'mmm', 'yes', 'I see' in such a way that the child knows that you are listening. The teacher should be guided by the child who will 'go in and out of grief'. Be there when needed and respond 'little and often'. Let a child or adolescent grieve in his own way. Note that some pupils show little emotion; this may be because the death has not sunk in.

It is helpful for children and adolescents to talk to others who knew their mother and have memories which are different from their own. These 'memory holders' can be encouraged to write down their stories for the bereaved pupil and give them to him. I remember when my youngest sister died, many of the condolence cards contained such stories; and they were a source of great comfort.

There may be one person to whom the child has turned for help during the time of mum's illness and final death. That person has had the trust of the child placed in them. Duffy comments on this:

> the strong relationship that will be built up between you over a period of time is to be treasured; it will always be part of you, and special. Make sure that the child knows where to get in touch with you at any time in the future – just in case for whatever reason, your reassurance is needed. (Duffy 2008, p.53)

Pastoral care responding to an incident in the media

This might be a car accident resulting in adults in the school, known to the pupils, being killed, or an accident involving a school bus with fatalities which effects the whole school. It is important for the administration to recognise the impact on pupils. Teachers will need information on trauma symptoms and know how to respond. In this sad event, how the children are told is very significant. It needs to recognise the media reports; pupils may need to share what they have been told about the accident and what they think actually happened, yet central is the grief which pupils and other staff will feel. It needs sensitivity. Time and silence will be needed.

There are international and national events where pupils have no personal involvement but are nonetheless, through the media and social networks, affected by them. Such an event arose from those fleeing from war in Syria to Europe by crossing the Mediterranean Sea in small boats at the hands of traffickers. On 3 September 2015, the international media was flooded with pictures of Aylan Kurdi, a three-year-old lying on the beach of a Greek island. As a police officer went towards the child, he prayed that this would not be the body of another migrant. The body of Alyan was cradled in his arms, the picture challenging the world to recognise the migrant crisis and the risks being faced. Children in school saw these pictures and wondered what they could do to help. Wendy Duffy comments on the importance of encouraging communication and openness in response to a situation like this cannot be overstated: parents need to feel confident that, in a crisis, the school has the interests of their child at heart and will respond to such crises with common sense and sensitivity in partnership with parents, to ensure that the message and support given is along the same lines (Duffy 2008, pp.45–6).

Pastoral care in response to the suicide of a pupil

An adolescent's experience is found at the beginning of Chapter 3 and indicates the significance of a school to such a sad incident. Thoughts of suicide arise within the child and adolescent due to a multitude of reasons and come within the remit of the Mental Health Services. In the UK only 0.6 per cent of the NHS budget is allocated to children and adolescents with mental health problems; waiting time for treatment can be six to nine months and in some cases two years. The prevalence of childhood depression is estimated to be 1 per cent in children in primary schools and 3 per cent in secondary schools and academies. Children show signs of sadness and helplessness through factors such as abuse and bullying. For example, a young child returning from a parental bereavement may be told by others in the playground, 'You can't join in because you haven't got a mother.' Adolescents may feel unloved and unfairly treated. They may experience cyber bullying, are encouraged to 'sext' until it is used against them by an ex-boyfriend and are sexually abused, each type of experience resulting in guilt and despair. Ten per cent of those with depression recover spontaneously within three months, 50 per cent remain clinically depressed at 12 months, and 20–30 per cent at two years. For parents who are concerned about depressive type behaviour in their child or adolescent, websites can help immediately and be a life-saver, giving a phone number for advice (see the Useful Websites and Organisations section). Some children, however, contemplate suicide.

I found no figures for child suicides, though they exist (see NICE Clinical Guidelines 2015). There is a prevalence of around 1–3 per cent for medically serious suicide attempts in adolescents and a substantial risk of recurrence of suicidal behaviour ranging from 5–15 per cent. Suicide can be preceded by self-harm injury on purpose such as burning oneself, overdosing, using drugs for highs, pulling hair or picking skin. This behaviour is an attempt to feel detached from the world and is a cry for help. Self-harm is a way of punishing the self which is often kept secret; clues may be the refusal to wear short sleeves or to take off clothing for a sports lesson. Other signs that a teenager has got to a deep place and is thinking of suicide may be ringing a friend to chat at 3am or listening to loud music. Some adolescents, such as Sandra, keep a journal of their most intimate thoughts, particularly if they are being bullied or are having feelings that they think are absurd and don't want anyone else to know about (see the adolescent experience in Chapter 3). The adolescent may contemplate suicide as the only way out. If his journal goes missing or another youngster picks it up, and the school has a robust ethos of pastoral care, then the youngster finding the journal is likely to tell a trusted teacher if he thinks a friend is in trouble, upset or showing signs of harming themselves. Friends may worry about betraying a confidence but self-harm can endanger lives and therefore should never be kept secret.

Many large secondary schools have a trained counsellor on the staff specialising in adolescent behaviour or can call in the outside resource of such a person. The head teacher may call in the parent and inform him about the evidence. A parent may be devastated by the news, having thought strange behaviour was normal adolescent growing up but be only too willing to receive the help the school can offer. On occasions a parent may refuse to believe, and must gently be shown the evidence and told the consequences of not acting. This area of school work is very sensitive and confidentiality is essential. A source of help is the website for the MindEd Trust (see the Useful Websites and Organisations section).

The suicide of a known adult

The suicide of a pupil's parent or close relative may evoke feelings of abandonment, shame and social stigma. Pupils affected need to know that they are not alone; be helped to learn how to manage anxiety and feelings of guilt; and have opportunities to talk openly to a teacher about why a person chooses to die by suicide. School may be the place where a child feels able to talk if the person who died by suicide is a parent. Sources of help are available (see Chapter 3, pages 76–79 and the Useful Websites and Organisations section).

School responses to incidents of bereavement – assembly

There are times when a grief is private. At other times, following the death of a child, or a teacher who was known by everyone in a primary school, it is helpful to come together for an assembly. This will be a time of quiet reflecting, remembering, thanking and celebrating the life of the deceased. It is important that the family of the person should be consulted. Pupils may well have ideas of what should be included in the assembly and might like to write or draw pictures of their memories, and fundraise to buy a permanent reminder of the deceased, chosen by the children. If appropriate invite the family to attend. The occasion needs to be sensitive to the faith culture of the pupils and be a positive experience, with a clear ritual beginning, a middle and a positive end.

On some occasions the assembly is very simple with a brief naming of the person and their significance to the pupils and staff, followed by several minutes of silence and quiet music. It could involve the ritual lighting of a candle, singing, listening to the favourite music of the deceased, prayers, reading poetry written by the children or memories written on paper leaves in the classroom and hung on the branch of a 'tree' during the assembly or stuck in a memory book for the family. At the end of the assembly, the leaves or memory box could be given, or sent, to the family, the remembrance candle blown out and balloons released outside with messages attached, for example. The school where my late sister worked planted a rose tree in her memory. It is useful to have playtime after such an assembly giving children time to assimilate what has happened before carrying on with the daily routine. Playtime can also be an occasion when children may use the member of staff on duty for reassurance or question what has happened.

It is important to be aware that some parents believe strongly that children should not be involved in anything to do with death and funerals. In a local primary school, an assembly was held to celebrate the life of one of the pupils who had died from a terminal illness. On hearing about the assembly, a parent rang the head teacher and berated him for subjecting her child to this experience. She believed that children were innocent of such things as death.

An assembly for adolescents

This will be different from the more intimate occasion in a primary or elementary school when the deceased was known by everyone. Secondary schools are large institutions and the deceased will not be known by the whole school. However, it is still appropriate to remember the deceased and celebrate memories in an assembly. The content could be organised by a small group supported by the advice of a member of staff. Those attending might be a year group or a house group, depending on the person remembered.

Pastoral care as a pupil returns to school after a bereavement

Sometimes a bereaved child or adolescent has time away from school following a death, needing to be with his family. Another child may want to return to the familiar pattern of the school routine quickly. There are likely, whichever time scale is appropriate, to be concerns about returning to school. A bereaved pupil may wonder, 'What do my friends and teacher know? How will they treat me? Should I talk about my dead parent?' The child may be fearful of his emotions and of being suddenly tearful or angry about what has happened at home. He may be concerned that he will have missed school work and not understand, nor be able to concentrate.

The class teacher can help in several ways, first, if possible by visiting the pupil at home or asking the pupil to come in one day after school so that decisions may be made and to reassure him of support. Second, the class teacher can help by preparing his fellow pupils. The former can be achieved by agreeing strategies if there is distress, such as a yellow 'exit' card, or a 'time out' card given to the pupil and carried in his pocket. The pupil shows it to a member of staff and has permission to leave the classroom, without being asked, when feeling upset, out of control or just to get 'personal space'. It is important that all staff teaching the pupil know about the card. It is essential that the pupil knows a designated place to go and that an adult will be there for as long as it is necessary. Simply having the card may act as a resource to the pupil who may then not need to use it.

A pupil can carry something small such as a shell or a pebble in a pocket as a comforter, which will be known only to him and the teacher. Holding onto something solid such as a pebble or a small shell can act as grounding, helping the pupil to feel in control if he is upset. A small picture of the deceased or a piece of fabric or garment that belonged to the deceased can provide a comforting memory. For a bereaved child or adolescent who finds it difficult to communicate, a small notebook can be used in which the child can write or draw what he is feeling. The pupil can leave this diary on the teacher's desk for the teacher to know, respond and return to its owner. Alternatively, the diary may be solely for the child's use. A young child may have a card with a happy face drawn on one side and a sad face on the other. The pupil can show the side that reflects what he is feeling that day and the teacher can respond. These are all helpful strategies a teacher can discuss with a pupil before he returns to school. See also the advice in the Childhood Bereavement UK section 'Supporting bereaved children and young people in school' on the website (see the Useful Websites and Organisations section).

The question of homework or missed work can be addressed by agreeing what is essential and what is not, or the teacher making a missed worksheet available, and the promise of extra help and support at some break times when needed. The class, in circle time in primary school or tutor time in secondary school, can be prepared for the return of their fellow pupil by exploring the thinking and feelings that emerge when a child loses something precious: what must it be like never finding the precious thing? This could be applied to the loss of a pet that wanders off and is lost, then thinking of the permanent loss of a parent. Some role play of feelings and being in someone else's shoes might be useful. The class could work out strategies of help and support and who would be the most suitable person to do this so that the bereaved pupil is not overwhelmed. The help should always be mindful of the pupil's wishes.

The child or adolescent's reactions to a death will vary depending on age, conceptual development, personality, relationship with the deceased and the nature of the death; each will be unique. There is no set pattern or time limit to grief. Table 5.1 shows the typical responses to death in school pupils. The pastoral care of pupils goes hand in hand with exploring and teaching through the school curriculum.

Table 5.1 Common responses to a death in school
pupils (The Dougy Center 2006)

Academic	Behavioural
Inability to focus or concentrate	Noisy outbursts, disruptive behaviours
Failing or declining grades	Aggressive behaviours, frequent fighting
Increased absences or reluctance to go to school	Non-compliance to requests
Forgetfulness, memory loss	Increase in risk taking or unsafe behaviour
Over achievement, trying to be perfect	Isolation or withdrawal
Language errors and word-finding problems	Regressive behaviours to a time when things felt more safe and in control
Inattentiveness	High need for attention
Daydreaming	A need for checking in on surviving parent(s)
Emotional	**Social**
Insecurity, issues of abandonment, safety concerns	Withdrawal from friends
Concern about being treated differently from others	Withdrawal from activities or sports
	Use of drugs or alcohol
Fear, guilt, anger, rage, regret, sadness, confusion	Changes in relationships with teachers and peers
'I don't care' attitude	Changes in family roles (taking on role of a deceased parent)
Depression, hopelessness, intense sadness	Wanting to be physically close to safe adults
Overly sensitive, frequently tearful, irritable	Sexually acting out
Appears unaffected by the death	Stealing, shoplifting
Preoccupation with death, wanting details	Difficulty with being in a group or crowd
Recurring thoughts of death or suicide	
Physical	**Spiritual**
Stomach aches, headaches, heartaches	Anger at God
Frequent accidents or injuries	Questions of 'Why me?' and 'Why now?'
Increased requests to visit the nurse	Questions about the meaning of life
Nightmare, dreams or sleep difficulties	Confusion about where the person who died is
Loss of appetite or increased eating	Feelings of being alone in the universe
Low energy, weakness	Doubting or questioning previous beliefs
Hives, rashes, itching	Sense of meaninglessness about the future
Nausea or upset stomach	Change in values, questioning what is important
Increased illness, low resistance to colds and flu	
Rapid heart beat	

Creating a policy for the school curriculum

First, it is important to discover if there are a clear rationale and aims for the exploration of loss through the curriculum. Second, it is necessary to question how these aims support the overall aims of the school. Third, it must be asked if there are clear principles for the exploration of loss, and fourth, how these principles support the principles of:

- access and entitlement

- curricular balance

- differentiation and potential

- preparation for the future.

The curriculum will be academic and intellectually rigorous but will also include the emotions and the social effects of loss.

The educational aspect of death and bereavement is likely to include the following: first knowledge, for example, the recognition of different losses, rites of passage, beginnings and endings, cultural differences, funeral practices and the irreversibility of death. Second, skills such as handling emotions and dealing with anger; third, positive attitudes, for example that death is natural and life is for living and enjoying.

It is helpful to have a teacher identified to coordinate work on loss within the school as this will allow a group of staff to plan work in a systematic way, making clear how different subjects and other curricular activities contribute to a growing awareness and understanding. The policy needs to make clear how work on loss is linked to bereavement support. It needs to indicate the range of resources available to support work, establish continuity and monitor and evaluate. Sensitive handling is needed since it is recognised that certain curriculum subjects may be difficult and bring up distressing memories for pupils.

The book *The Meaning of Death* (Feifel 1959) noted that the subject of death had become taboo in the twentieth century in the USA. The author challenged individuals to recognise their mortality, suggesting that this was essential to live a meaningful life in the present. Later studies showed that children also grieve and can benefit from support, so programmes for bereaved children were established. The Dougy Center, a community-based volunteer programme in Portland, Oregon was founded in 1985, becoming a model and training centre for professionals across the nation and creating grief support programmes for children.

The principle aims of 'Death Education' in the USA curriculum are to promote quality of life for oneself and others, and assist in creating and maintaining the conditions that achieve this. 'Death Education' varies in goals, format, duration, intensity and characteristics of participants. It can be formal or informal and offered at elementary, middle and high school levels. Informally it arises through occasions in the home recognised as 'teachable moments', such as the birth of a sibling and the death of a pet, which naturally lead to interactions that answer the child's questions about life. In school there are two distinct methods: first, the didactic using lectures and audiovisuals to improve knowledge; and second, the experiential, actively involving pupils by evoking feelings and allowing death-related attitudes to be modified. It includes personal sharing of experiences in group discussion, role play and simulation exercises and requires pupils' mutual trust. Most teachers use a combination of the two approaches. Children have fears and concerns about death, yet studies of older children with life-threatening illnesses show that by giving information about diagnosis, prognosis and treatment options, death anxiety is lowered, creating a measure of control. This may also be true of healthy children. Improved information and discussion about the consequences of risk taking in adolescents may reduce existing death anxiety and help prevent risk-taking behaviour. In the UK, Spiritual, Moral, Social and Cultural (SMSC) development runs throughout the whole curriculum, defined, by the government Department for Education (DfE) for schools and Ofsted education inspectors, as subject matter to 'explore beliefs and experience; respect faiths, feelings and values; enjoy learning about oneself, others and the surrounding world; use imagination and creativity and reflect' (DfE 2014). Inspectors look for some element of SMSC in every lesson, which is problematic when teaching maths. From November 2014, schools are supposed to promote 'British' values through SMSC, and since 1 July 2015, schools have had a legal duty to prevent pupils from being radicalised. Since September 2015, SMSC has been compulsory and inspected. In secondary schools, the Department for Education recommend using the citizenship curriculum for this. Schools have taught citizenship since 2002. It parallels SMSC in 'appreciating diversity, understanding different viewpoints and collaborating for change' (Doing SMSC n.d.). SMSC will naturally be a place topics around loss, bereavement and death occur.

Key Stage 1 (5–7 years)

At this age children generally experience small losses – a milk tooth, a broken toy, a cancelled outing and the death of a classroom pet. They will be aware of seasonal changes and of life cycles in insects, for example caterpillars into butterflies, spawn into tadpoles and frogs, and perhaps the scan indicating the growth of a potential sibling. These areas of learning will happen through observation, recording, nature study, science and story. Emotions at loss will be expressed, leading to the burial of a dead classroom pet with rituals created. Stories are helpful since they are objective and children can identify with the characters and the plot. Literature is a significant resource to help young children explore challenging areas of life (see the age-appropriate suggestions in the Further Reading section at the end of the book).

Key Stage 2 (7–11 years)

At this age children are able to take more responsibility. They are still concrete thinkers. The curriculum will use music, movement and dance to explore feelings and moods; English can involve writing letters to comfort others and listening to stories; and in history children can visit churches and graveyards to look at words on gravestones and dates of birth and death (maths could be used here). Learning about the two World Wars and others since and the commemorations of Remembrance Day is important. A 'memory tree' could be made in art and design, for example, with each pupil drawing a tree to represent themselves. Ask imaginative questions such as, 'What sort of tree are you – an oak, a weeping willow, a silver birch?' It is important to let the child decide. The height of the tree shows the age of the pupil. Show the roots and the branches. Think about the soil that the tree is growing in, is it good and nourishing? How can the soil be improved? Think about the losses in life and draw them as branches, the lower ones representing the first losses. What were these losses? The pupil might like to write the losses on the branches – for example, the loss of milk teeth, a pet that has died, a change of school or parents parting can all be included. The child's sadness can be shown by leaves falling from the branches. Sometimes new life can come from a loss – represent this with a new branch. Then encourage the pupil to think of the good things that have happened – the first bike, having a pair of roller skates or a skateboard, hiking and joining the cubs. These things the pupil enjoys can be shown by flowers or fruit with a word written on them or at the side.

This exercise may bring up challenging feelings so the teacher must be very sensitive. The exercise can be made over several sessions, ending each session with either a good thing that has happened that day or a serialised story of living with life and its challenges. (This activity has been developed from a suggestion in *The Child Bereavement Trust Workbook* 2000, pp.23–24.)

Key Stage 3 (11–14 years)

At 11 years old, children move from primary school to secondary. Emotionally mood swings denote the beginnings of puberty – the loss of childhood and movement towards adulthood, yet the loss of being the oldest in a small school to being the youngest in a large school. The curriculum becomes more segmented and specialised. Work in English could look at the purpose of literature and writing poetry, reading the war poets such as Wilfred Owen and Siegfried Sassoon. A visit to the war fields of the continent is often made at this age.

Key Stage 4 (14–16 years)

These two years are for most young people spent in preparing for external examinations, though subjects on the curriculum can introduce topics related to death and dying. Ideas can be found on the website Dying Matters (see the Useful Websites and Organisations section at the end of the book). This website includes lesson plans and curriculum links. Subjects such as English, where pupils study Shakespeare's 'Romeo and Juliet', could lead to a discussion on aspiration in life and death. Geography lessons could study the reasons why death rates and age of death vary so much across countries and include the implications of ageing populations in the developed world. History could well be a platform for discussing immigration within changing populations and religious studies will include work on rituals and faith beliefs.

Key Stage 5 (16–19 years)

At this age many pupils will be involved in vocational type training in further education colleges. These colleges will inevitably raise some of the big questions, such as an individual's gifts and inclinations, the purpose of work, the balance of job satisfaction and pay, working as an individual and working as part of a team. Other pupils will be involved in structured courses in preparation for external public exams and university applications. These pupils will encounter issues of independent study, research methods, planning time, the balance of study and leisure, future plans and priorities for their own lives. Many of these issues are related to ultimate questions such as the purpose in life.

Resources

Child Bereavement UK produce a folder 'Supporting Bereaved Children and Young People in School' as a free Schools Information Pack, though as they are a charity a donation is useful to them. The pack includes such subjects as how schools can help; responding to a death; supporting a bereaved pupil; parents and carers; how to put together a school policy; children's understanding of death; pupils with a life threatening illness; death through suicide; different cultures and beliefs; books for the various Key Stages and resources for staff – interestingly there was nothing specifically on the inclusion of material on death in the curriculum, yet this would be a response to the Department for Education SMCS requirement and respond to the questioning and experience of children.

There is a useful website for Schoolswork (see the Useful Websites and Organisations section), which aims to help schools in a pastoral capacity.

Believers' experiences – world faiths

In our schools there are children from different faith backgrounds and from none. In parts of the UK, teachers will meet Muslim children. When helping a bereaved child or adolescent it is helpful to know his faith background and if possible to be in contact with the local faith communities, if any, to enable the care and support of pupils.

Faith schools are a significant feature of the UK education system. The Anglican Church pioneered universal education. The two main providers in England are the Church of England and the Catholic

Education Service. Until 1997, the UK funded only Christian schools. Jewish and Muslim schools existed but were privately funded. In 2011, about a third of the 20,000 schools in England were faith schools, about 7000 in total; 68 per cent were Church of England, 30 per cent were Roman Catholic, 42 were Jewish, 12 Muslim, three Sikh and one Hindu (Office for National Statistics 2011). These are the latest percentages available and are likely to distort the number of Muslim schools now in existence. Muslims also educate their young in an after-school Qur'an school, a *Madrasah*; there are 700 in Britain attended by 100,000 children of Muslim parents. The *Madrasah* associated with the Hifdh branch of Islam state:

> Our aim is to educate and prepare the younger generation…through knowledge, wisdom, good morals and manners using successful methods existing in the Qur'an…moulding the future generations… who by the permission of Allah will become model British citizens and beacons of light in the wider society.

Church schools are either voluntary controlled (VC) or voluntary aided (VA). In 1998, 'foundation' schools were introduced and in 2002, academies (state-funded independent schools). These were expanded in 2010 when existing schools were allowed to convert to academy status and 'free schools' were introduced. In the British education system for historic reasons religious education and an act of worship are compulsory. A faith school teaches a general curriculum, but has a particular religious character, which emerges from its origin in a religious organisation, while being state funded.

Following the 2010 Academy Act, many schools converted to Academy status and are sometimes known as 'faith academies', as are free schools with a religious designation. Academies are not obliged to follow the National Curriculum. However, Michael Gove, the then Education Secretary, stated the teaching of creationism is at odds with scientific fact: the Department for Education 'will not approve any application where we have any concern about creationism being taught as a valid scientific theory, or about schools failing to teach evolution adequately as part of their science curricula' (Butt 2014). Since 2014, racist propaganda in schools can be prosecuted. Faith schools give priority of admission to those connected with their faith, though if state funded they admit other applicants if they cannot fill their places and must comply with the School Admissions Code. Since education is a devolved matter, it differs in Scotland and Northern Ireland. Local priests are on the management board of Church primary schools and the governing board of Church secondary schools and can be supportive to staff as staff are supportive to children.

Faith schools are not without their critics. The British Humanist Association and National Secular Society have campaigned that faith schools teach a broader range of beliefs in society. *The Guardian* newspaper criticised faith schools for selecting pupils only from well-off families (Shepherd and Rogers 2012). In 2005, the Office for Standards in Education (Ofsted) noted that faith schools should be carefully but sensitively monitored by government to ensure pupils receive an understanding of not only their own faith but others and the wider tenets of British society. A 2006 article in *The Guardian* highlighted abuse in faith schools: Britain's 700 unregulated madrasas need to be monitored nationally to stop children being exposed to significant physical and sexual abuse, a Muslim body has warned. The Muslim parliament of Great Britain will today urge the government to set up a national register for the mosque schools, coordinated and monitored by local authorities, to meet their local obligations the Children Act 1989 (Smith 2006). In June 2013, the Fair Admissions Campaign was launched, supported by religious and non-religious organisations and educationalists. In October 2013, the Theos Think Tank produced *More than an Educated Guess: Assessing the Evidence on Faith School* (Oldfield, Hartnett and Bailey 2013). The report recognises the Church as pioneer of mass education in Britain, but states that within the education sector faith schools have become contentious. In 2015, further concerns about standards have been expressed, nevertheless faith schools and academies are a significant contribution to the British educational system. The teaching of religion has changed, as has its name from 'scripture' or 'religious instruction' to 'religious education'. In Wales the subject has been renamed 'religion, philosophy and ethics'. The 1988 Education Reform Act continued the requirement that it should be compulsory but defined it as a component in the 'basic curriculum', not the National Curriculum. It also required that in schools without a religious character attention should be given to all the principal religions of the UK, not only to Christianity.

A Commission on Religion and Belief in British Public Life was convened in 2013 by the Woolf Institute in Cambridge and was reported on 7 December 2015. The report *Living with Difference*

(Commission on Religion and Belief in British Public Life 2015) refers to the above matters in its Chapter 4, 'Education'. The report recognises:

> If the place of religion and belief in British public life is to be better understood, and if a society that works for the common good is to be achieved, it is vital to give attention to what is taught and learnt about religion and belief in schools…both formal and non-formal. (p.30)

The report takes issue with the admission policy of Church schools, stating they are selective of the middle class who are determined to get their children into a Church school and can move house in order to do so. This is only partly true since Church schools are popular because of their high standards and achievements, reported in Ofsted inspections, and are sought by Muslim parents in urban areas since the stance of the school promotes particular, more spiritual, values.

On the question of the teaching of religious education, Church schools have a broad syllabus of enquiry, and respecting and exploring the major faiths is part of the school assembly. This is important as the Report states that children should be brought together to share their faiths, and within Church schools there is a recognition of the diversity of pupils' home backgrounds. There are challenges with education, for example the number of Agreed Syllabuses for the teaching of religious education, but this needs to be addressed by all. Questions continue to be addressed by Church and State.

Drawing together experience and cultural context leading to practical implications

Many teachers want to help a child and adolescent coping with issues around death and dying, but feel anxious about supporting children in their care and fear saying the wrong thing. On the other hand, sometimes children and young people may want to talk openly about what is happening at home, but find that those around them avoid the issue. There is no one-size-fits-all solution. Teachers need to adjust their approach to different children.

In schools, work on loss may feature in informal ways. Primary school children gather in a circle at the end of a school day. Children sit around the teacher to share news, discuss something they have seen on the TV or listen to a story. This may well include a topical event which raises questions for children. Adolescents spend useful time listening to one another in tutor time. Grieving pupils talk to members of staff, in incidental conversations, for example in the dinner queue, before lessons and following something said in assembly.

The curriculum is significant in enabling pupils to explore important issues around death and bereavement, which are part of life to be faced and incorporated into life's meaning.

ACTIVITIES TO ELICIT THE READER'S EXPERIENCE

A book review – pick up a book intended for a pupil you know on the subject of death or bereavement. Read it. Write a paragraph of reflections showing how you would use the book or why you consider it unsuitable.

6

Funerals
The Attendance and Participation of Children and Adolescents

When you go to heaven are you still the same person you were? If you had a limp do you still have one in heaven or do you become new?

(Cynthia in Marshall 2003, p.46)

A child's experience

Betsy and Barbara were sisters. They attended primary school. Their favourite grandad had died and they were very sad. They asked their parents where he was and were told that his body was with the funeral director who would prepare it for the funeral. After the funeral, his body would be cremated. Neither girl had heard of cremation. Their parents said that cremation meant that his body would be burnt. At this, the two girls shrieked in horror, rushed upstairs and disappeared into their respective bedrooms crying loudly, slamming the doors behind them. Neither would talk to their parents, adults who would let this horrendous thing happen.

Reflection on experience

It is important that children understand what happens when someone dies, at a funeral and afterwards when the body is buried or cremated. The particular behaviour here originated in the lack of discussion around death and the lack of understanding that at death the physical body is no longer working and the functions of the body cease. A friend of mine talked about the ashes from a cremation as 'divine compost'. In the book, *The Tenth Good Thing About Barney*, the cat's young owner discovers that when Barney is buried in the ground, his body changes and Barney becomes like compost and will help 'grow flowers. You know, I said, that's a pretty nice job for a cat' (Viorst 1988, p.24). A dead body is without life and cannot feel heat or pain. Fire at cremation is very hot, burns the body and turns it into a fine powder.

An adolescent's experience

Three young men were killed on motorbikes on a wet, windy night by sliding into one another going too fast round a bend. It was a rural area and the lads were well known. Their fellow bikers were distraught when they heard what had happened and wanted to do something to express their own grief and sadness and offer their condolences and solidarity with the family in their grief. With the permission of the family, and working together with the priest, the bikers made a rota and kept an all-night vigil with candles around the coffins of their friends the night before the funeral.

Reflection on experience

These seemingly tough young lads showed physical emotions when the death was 'one of their own'. This is in a context and culture where 'men don't cry'. They wanted to show their respect and solidarity with the families of their mates. Fortunately, it was possible for them to work together with the families and the local priest, helping thems to grieve without realising and showing respect, and solidarity with the bereaved families.

Linking adult, child and adolescent experience

Children and young people are not fazed by death when they experience it, if they are helped with explanations when they have questions. It is adults, in the UK particularly, who continue to treat death as a taboo subject and extend this by attempting to protect their young children, thinking that children are innocent of such events. Adolescents are much more like adults in their acceptance of death.

Sociological, psychological and historical insights

For centuries the whole life cycle in the West, birth to death, happened in the home. Babies were born in the home and families usually washed and cared for their dead at home. The family would come into the room where the body was, often in an open coffin. The body remained at home for viewing by neighbours and friends until the funeral which all, including children, would attend. This continues to be so in remote rural areas and in the developing world. Today it is very different. Most people die in hospital or a care home, and the body is cared for and stored by the funeral director, a stranger to the deceased and to the family. The statistics of the place of death are (Office of National Statistics 2011):

- 5 per cent hospices (NHS and non NHS)

- 18 per cent residential homes (Local Authority and private)

- 21 per cent home

- 53 per cent hospital.

Many adults have never seen a dead body.

What happens when someone dies?

It is important to explain to children what happens when someone dies in words appropriate for their stage of conceptual development, particularly if the deceased is a close family member, a parent, a sibling or a favourite grandparent (see Chapter 4). Young children understand literally, so using expressions such as the euphemisms, 'We've lost your mum', or 'Grandad's gone away' need to be avoided. Children can be told that the person doesn't need their body any more. It has worn out. They cannot feel any pain. They don't need food or air nor are they lonely. The body is taken by men and women called undertakers to a mortuary, where it is made ready for a special ceremony called a funeral. The body is washed and dressed, the hair is combed and make up applied. It is usually dressed in clothes provided by the family.

The body is put in a box of wood or sometimes thick cardboard or woven branches, which has handles and usually a lid and is especially made for the deceased. The box is called a coffin. The idea of being put in a box and buried or burned can be frightening to a child whereas as adults we take it for granted. Listening carefully to children's questions and giving clear explanations are essential. For young children the book *Autumn: Betsy Bear Learns About Death* is helpful (Francis and Slee 1996). An older child may be helped by thinking about what we do with leaves in autumn. The leaves are no longer needed, so we put them in a black bin bag and allow them to disintegrate and turn into compost. Or we burn the leaves and turn them into ashes, which is used for compost.

The funeral directors have a Chapel of Rest in which the coffin can be placed on a table and the family of the deceased can visit. Some families do not visit and certainly do not want the children to see the body after death nor attend the funeral, but children know about endings from seeing a dead bird in the garden or at the side of a road. Should children see the dead body of someone who has been close to them? There is no right or wrong answer; it depends on the feelings of the parents or carers and the children themselves. Visiting the Chapel of Rest can help children realise the finality of death and be less scared. Children are usually more scared about what they don't know than what they do. Not knowing is an opportunity for their imagination to run riot. Allowing children to visit helps them feel included and enables them to say goodbye. The funeral directors can advise, and if they know that children are coming to view, they may be very helpful in adding words to parental explanations. Some funeral companies produce booklets for children, for example, Dignity

Caring Funerals. The chapel is also a private place. A correspondent to a *Guardian* newspaper article wrote:

> My father-in-law died when my son was four. He was very fond of this grandfather and when the family went to see the open coffin everyone said not to let the children into the room. We asked our son what he wanted to do, and he wanted to come in with us, so he did. His reactions? 'That his grandfather looked nice and peaceful, as if he were asleep.' It was all very natural and a good way to say 'adieu'. (Hilpern 2013)

Another respondent recorded a three-year-old who was very fond of her next-door neighbours. When the man died, his wife and her friend, both ex-nurses, had laid out her dead husband in the bedroom. The child and mother went to offer their sorrow at the death, the widow commented:

> The three year old asked if she could see him, and her mother, rather reluctantly, took her upstairs. She stood for a moment looking at him and said, 'he can't see me and he can't hear me, can he?' Her mother agreed that this was so. She gave a sigh and turned to come back downstairs, smiled at me and went home quite calmly. (Hilpern 2013)

If children want to see the dead body, it is important to tell them what they are likely to see. It helps to tell them that sometimes when a person dies their friends and family go and say goodbye. The body is in a big box called a coffin. The body is the part that is left, but the part that is special about the person, her spirit and the memories we have her, will last for ever. The body won't be like it used to be. The person can no longer talk or walk or sleep, nor need to eat. The body might feel cold and look pale, a bit like wax.

John was six. He was not told when he visited his gran in hospital that she was dying. Gran had lived with the family since John was a small child. When he started going to school he would run home and tell his gran all that had happened. Just after the family returned home from the hospital, a phone call to the parents said that she had died. John realised from his parents' expressions that something had happened and insisted on finding out what the hospital had said. When told, John did not believe his gran had died, since he believed that hospitals made people better. This incident made it very difficult to convince John that his gran was actually dead. His parents told him that she was old and that her body had gradually stopped working. John wanted to see her. A friend suggested that the funeral director be consulted before his parents considered taking John to see his gran at the Chapel of Rest. His parents repeated what he would see when he got to the funeral parlour but John insisted. The experience in the Chapel of Rest helped John to understand what death is and he decided to go into the local church so that he could light a candle to remember his gran.

If a child wants to see the body, she can be told that in the Chapel of Rest it is fine to go and to touch the body, or kiss it or simply stand at the door. If necessary, and the child gets upset, she can leave early and go outside with an adult. It is fine if the child says she does not want to see the body. It is useful to assure the child that many other families prefer not to go to the Chapel of Rest, but to remember the person when they were alive, then it can be suggested that she might like to draw a picture or write a poem or memories of the deceased and that these can be put into the coffin. If the family attend the Chapel of Rest leaving a child behind, she may feel excluded or think that death is too horrible to see.

Why funerals?

A funeral is a ritual, a rite of passage. Young children are likely to have felt sadness, confusion or even guilt for not caring following the death of a precious pet at home, at kindergarten or nursery school. They may have experienced a funeral for the pet, perhaps digging a hole for the body, reciting memories of the deceased pet and marking the grave with a lolly stick cross with great ceremony. Children revel in such ceremony and ritual. Some parents simply hide the pet's body from the child, replace the dead pet with another animal, hoping the child won't notice. This cheats the child of the reality of death, an event that is natural and part of life. The book, *The Tenth Good Thing About Barney* is the story of the funeral of a cat (Viorst 1988). The purpose of a funeral is something that children can engage with, since even young children can understand beginnings and endings. Duffy comments that adults 'forget that they (children) too must experience the fact of death otherwise they are left in an unresolved void' (Duffy 2008, p.52). A useful story book on beginnings and endings is *The Giving Tree* (Silverstein 1964), and a good factual book is *Lifetimes* (Mellonie and Ingpen 1983). A funeral is about saying goodbye and honouring the deceased through, as a community of the bereaved, sharing sadness and joyful memories of the significance of this person. It is to recognise, for a child at a parent's death, that a change has taken place, which for a child means the regaining of confidence lost when somehow she felt they were responsible for the death. It is the recognition for a child that life does not end in death, since there are memories of the deceased. For some adults, the funeral is closure, but children will revisit memories at key events in their lives, such as going to high school, passing external exams, going to college or university, since the loved one will not be present to share the event with them. The memoires may be what the deceased taught the child, from tying shoe laces to learning to fish. A useful book for young children on memories of the loved one is *Badger's Parting Gifts* (Varley 1984, 1992). For others, the funeral will be about a belief in an afterlife, which is sometimes a religious belief such as a concept of heaven.

Should children attend a funeral?

The British Social Attitudes Survey of May 2013 showed that 48 per cent of adults still think it is inappropriate for children under 12 to attend funerals, yet research in the USA has shown that attendance at funerals and viewing the body can have long-term benefits for children (Hilpern 2013).

From about six years onwards, children should not be forced but given, as a right, the decision of choosing whether or not to attend a funeral. Children should be told what they will see and what they should expect. For very young children, up to five years of age, the parent can generally decide what would be best, when it is the funeral of a parent, sibling, grandparent or close friend. Being shut out is far more damaging, being hidden and unknown, than facing a new and possibly difficult experience with loving support.

Michael Morpurgo wrote of his first experience of death: that of his grandfather, which happened while he was a child at boarding school. He was told the news by the headmaster and that he should have the morning off lessons. He took a long walk, remembered but didn't cry, though he commented later:

> I never went to see him. I never went to the funeral. I never said goodbye properly…his death remained unreal and remains unreal… death and dying continued to haunt me. And I'm sure now the fear

was the fear of the unknown, would it hurt? Would I go to hell? Or would I just drift off into the blackness of eternity or infinity? (Morpurgo 2006, p.5)

Years later he saw the body when his grandmother died. 'This time I did get to say goodbye. As I looked down on her I simply thought: this is all death is, the end of the story...We need intimations of mortality' (p.5).

A funeral enables a child to feel part of a grieving community and relieves her sense of aloneness. The child sees that other people loved the deceased and are as sad as she is. If it is the funeral of the child's parent, there may be school teachers present and other pupils; the bereaved child then feels affirmed and encouraged. A child losing a parent may feel deserted but attending the funeral can help the child feel important at a time when he or she may feel displaced by what is happening around them. Duffy comments, 'Years later a child can look back and be glad that they were included in an important family occasion' (Duffy 2008, p.52).

A seven-year-old was not told of his grandad's death or funeral. Grandad just 'disappeared' from his life. He harboured resentment of his parents' stance until his adulthood. Another ten-year-old, Emma, said:

My dad died suddenly...one day we were on holiday and everything was normal, the next thing I knew, he disappeared from my life. To have gone to his funeral would have acknowledged that and given me a chance to say goodbye. (Hilpern 2013)

As a late teenager she started having panic attacks at funerals and sought counselling: 'I was finally grieving for my dad...not going to his funeral was a major influence.' Her mother suffered enormous guilt over the years, saying:

the problem with an unexpected death is that you're in shock and not thinking straight...and you only have days to make decisions about the funeral...I decided the right thing was for Emma not to go because I wanted to protect her...but quickly regretted it... not least because I know what it has cost her over the years...the crematorium was packed and Emma would have seen how much her dad was thought of. I now very firmly believe that she shouldn't just

have been there, she should have been involved in every part of it.
(Hilpern 2013)

Does stopping a child attending a funeral reflect adult insecurity
rather than children's fears? Children are resilient. A resource to help
in decision making and what to say to children is 'Talking to children
about dying', which is free to download from the Dying Matters
website (see the Useful Websites and Organisations section).

It is important to know what might happen at a funeral. There
will be tears among some of the adults, but children don't normally
see adults crying. It is important that they do and realise that crying
is a positive thing that can help a person feel better, since it provides
a release for difficult feelings. If children see it's alright for adults to
cry, they are given permission to show their emotions. Adults may also
laugh at a funeral – this may arise from a memory recounted in the
eulogy, for instance – children must see it's OK to laugh too. If a child
does not want to attend a funeral, or parents don't think it suitable, this
must be honoured. There are alternatives. If the coffin is a cardboard
one it can be decorated by the children. Vikki Evans recounted how
her children aged four and three decorated a coffin with handprints
and glitter for their grandpa. The grandchildren had no false notions
about his passing; they know once a person dies he is gone for ever.
But they also understood that they had had a wonderful relationship
with that loved one, filled with experiences they would remember for
ever (Hilpern 2013). The children were told about his internment – he
did not want a funeral – but 'they were unfazed'. They were asked
what they would wear at the ceremony – something Grandpa would
have liked, they were told. The older girl chose a beautiful party dress,
the younger boy dressed as a knight in armour. Their mother said,
'They had given my father a work of art to sleep in, something from
which my mother, sister and I all drew comfort.' The article ends:

> since my father's; funeral, my children have been happy to chat about
> death – to anyone willing to listen, It hasn't stopped the panicky
> obligatory childhood sobs pleading with me and their father not to
> die – I think all children go through that stage. But maybe that's
> the point, I want my children to have a healthy understanding that
> death is inevitable and that it's OK to grieve however they want.
> (Hilpern 2013)

On occasions the school might help. Being aware of the date and time of the funeral, a sensitive adult, for example a classroom assistant, might take a bereaved child out of class to a quiet place, light a candle and let her talk about the deceased. If she would like to say an appropriate prayer or give thanks, the Lord's Prayer or another prayer could be said while the funeral is taking place. To share with children who do not attend, adults can make a recording of the funeral, take photos or have a video made. A list can be made of everyone present and these can be part of a memory book of the loved one, shared at special times, such as later at the birthday of the deceased.

Preparation for the funeral service

Adults are kept very busy after a death in planning the funeral and simple activities with the children can be done with a sensitive visitor, a known neighbour or a more distant relative. There are many ways of involving children creatively at times of loss; working at making things at these times is very valuable, allowing children to express the inexpressible, with no need for vocabulary which they may not yet have access to. The activities can be those children do all the time, so they are not threatening, such as painting, tearing, cutting and sticking. It is also a way to break the ice, since the process of creating something is a distraction which can allow fears, anxieties, observations and questions to be expressed naturally. The process is as important as the completion of the activity, since when a chance conversation arises it helps a child to realise that others are thinking of her and the deceased. Giving children choices about small things can also help them to feel they have some control in a situation which to them feels very uncontrollable. For example, children can be involved in choosing a favourite story such as *The Very Hungry Caterpillar* (Carle 2002) or *Badger's Parting Gifts* (Varley 1984) and making a list of attributes of Dad to add to the eulogy, such as Dad's special gifts were 'teaching me to cross the road safely', 'helping me learn to read', 'playing football with me and my mates'.

Children could cut some tall twigs on which to hang leaf-shaped tags in the deceased's favourite colour. As they come into the funeral, mourners could be given a leaf to write a memory on, the children collecting and hanging them on the tree during the service. Later they could be put in a decorated box and brought out on special occasions such as anniversaries. An alternative is for children to design a memory card to give out at the funeral for mourners to fill in, which can be collected and later pasted into a memory book.

Depending on the season, children could pot up bulbs or seeds and hand them out to mourners at the end of the service. I heard of a family whose young mother had died after a long struggle with cancer. There were sunflowers on her coffin, and as family and friends left the service, the young sons handed to everyone an envelope in which was a sunflower seed to grow and so remember her.

Children could make simple kites from supermarket bin bags decorating them with patterns using acrylic paint using a design or picture linked to a memory of the deceased and adding a tail. Another possible material is coloured tissue paper. As young children 'puddle jump' in and out of grief, it is useful to have something to play or run around with after a funeral.

Children can be prepared for a funeral by being told before what happens, who is responsible and where a funeral takes place. It can be explained as a special time of remembering with music, words, poems and a special talk, a tribute called a eulogy, about the person who has died. The occasion is led by a person who might be a church official, a minister, priest or lay Christian, the cultural leader of the faith of the family, a non-religious person, such as a humanist celebrant or a member of the bereaved family.

It is helpful to children particularly, if the person taking the rite spends time with the family. The family, including the children, could choose the words and music for the service. An understanding celebrant can take the family through the service, explaining what will happen. If children are to be present at the funeral, they might write a memory or a poem or draw a picture to go into the coffin.

Children can be told that the funeral takes place in a religious building, or a crematorium or outside on a greenfield site. It is important that a child is accompanied by a close family member or special friend who can be there for her afterwards. This alleviates the sense of being alone and allows a parent to express her grief for a deceased partner, child or her own parent. The coffin with the dead person will be brought in at the beginning. A heartbroken family need words of comfort knowing that the deceased will be remembered. At the service children could hand out service sheets as people come in or light candles at the beginning of the service.

Burial or cremation?

Explanations of why the body is buried or cremated will help to dispel any myths that children have. A six-year-old thought that God lived in the ground. When asked by a teacher why, she replied, 'Well, when people die they are put in the ground, and we say they are with God.' If possible, children should be shown before the funeral where the grave is or what happens to the ashes. A burial might be in a greenfield site, an ecological area, a specially designated area of grass and trees, a churchyard or a local authority site. Children can be told that the coffin will be taken to the burial ground in a special car called a hearse, which leads the procession of mourners' cars. It will be buried alongside other graves containing the coffins with bodies of other people someone loved. A large hole will have been cut in the ground, so that whoever carries the coffin lays it beside the hole, while mourners gather round. Words and prayers are said before the coffin is gently lowered into the ground. The family may throw handfuls of soil on the coffin, some scatter flower petals. The wreaths of flowers sent by people who knew the deceased are laid beside the grave. There is then likely to be a quiet time when those attending the burial look at the flowers and talk quietly. The funeral directors then let their men fill the hole with soil. A temporary marker of wood shows where the grave is. Some months later the family may have a stone carved with the name and dates of the deceased with a verse added. The grave is a permanent memory, later visited by family. Customs vary. Some families put fresh flowers on a grave at Easter, a time of the renewal of life; others on the anniversary of the death or the birth of the deceased. Others plant bulbs or small plants. The rules about this are determined by the local authorities that maintain the graveyard.

Families may decide that the body of the deceased should be cremated. Children can be told that the crematorium has huge ovens in which the coffin is placed and burnt until it becomes ashes. The ashes might be placed in a casket and kept in a family home, buried in a churchyard, scattered at sea or on a favourite walk of the deceased. The latter means that it there is no 'permanent' place to mourn; it is known only by the family. My youngest sister's body was cremated and her ashes scattered on her favourite secluded footpath overlooking the river. She asked for cremation, since she wanted to be free from the disease that had limited her. The whole family, including her teenage daughter and young cousins, helped scatter the ashes.

Later, my brother-in-law planted bulbs at the spot. A close friend was disappointed that there was not a public place such as an accessible churchyard in which to grieve.

The 'get together' after the funeral

Frequently, the family and other visitors get together after the funeral, which is difficult for children, since their memories will be different from the adults present who will have known the deceased longer as a relative, work mate or leisure companion. Even with family members, a child may not have met all the relatives and can feel left out. Sharon, 13, wrote, 'I feel I have the memories I have and the other people have no right to tell me they have any more. I don't know what to say to them. My own memories are very special' (Duffy 2008, p.53). A way through this is to give the child or adolescent a task, for example to write a list of attendees at the get together after the funeral and get each person to sign it. Or she could be asked to help with handing out sandwiches and drinks, or to get everyone to write down their memory of the deceased on a tag. A useful resource with a wealth of creative and imaginative ideas is *Children at Funerals* (Burgess 2003).

A 'wake' refers to the Irish way of handling life after a funeral. The wake is a traditional Irish custom, though it is ceasing to exist in cities and is even modified in country areas. The wake is the practice of continuously watching over the deceased from the time of death until the funeral. The origin of the wake may be the ancient Jewish custom of leaving the burial chamber or sepulchre unsealed for three days before finally closing it up, allowing the spirit of the person to leave. An alternative understanding of the origin is the custom of family members frequently visiting, in the hope that the deceased would show signs of a return to life. The word 'wake' comes from an Old English word meaning 'to bring to life; to stir' in the hope that the deceased will awake. Typically, the body is 'waked' for three days, usually in the deceased's home, with an open coffin allowing neighbours, distant friends and family to visit and pay their respects. The response to an article in *The Guardian* by a Northern Irish man was that he could not understand the taboo of talking about death in English culture, 'young or not we all went to funerals, and the wakes before, where the corpse was laid out...including, on one occasion a schoolmate' (Hilpern 2013). The man remembered that a favourite walk in his childhood was for him and his siblings to accompany their mother on a Sunday on the three miles to visit the family graves and to tend them: 'you could reconstruct the population of our streets from reading the tombstones, and as you grew older, more and more of the people you knew as a child started populating the graveyard' (Hilpern 2013). Another Irish correspondent said:

> I think the Irish tradition of a full-on, three day wake in an open house with catering, music and an open coffin is just about the healthiest way to kick-off the process of coming to terms with the loss of a loved one – and a brilliant way to show kids that life goes on. (Hilpern 2013)

Believers' experiences – world faiths

Judaism

After a death, the first person to call is the deceased's rabbi. A *Shomer* or 'watchman' stays with the deceased from death until the funeral and burial. The rabbi coordinates the needs of the family, his own time and that of the cemetery. In respect to the deceased and the mourners, traditionally Jewish funerals are held as soon after death as possible. A service may be held in the synagogue, though today many are opting for a service only at the cemetery. Choosing a casket for the body is difficult since it is the last thing to be purchased for the loved one. The service itself lasts about 20 minutes and consists of reciting psalms, reading Scripture and a eulogy. The *Kaddish* prayer is recited after the lowering of the casket and the grave has been filled with earth. Mourning continues in the home (see Chapter 2) and visits to the cemetery, but these visits are infrequent less the deceased be 'deified'.

Christianity

My youngest sister died just before Christmas in the hospice where I worked. Her death was expected. Most of the family were with her when she died. Angie left a bewildered husband and a fourteen-year-old daughter. Since it was near Christmas the family decided to have a funeral led by one of my colleagues in the church where Angie had been married and she and her daughter christened, but not to announce it publicly, since her husband and daughter could not cope with too many people. It was a service with a wicker, boat-shaped coffin, symbolic of the journey she was now on, Advent hymns, prayers, a committal to the God she loved and served and a Celtic blessing. We knew and said that our Angie was now singing with the angels in God's nearer presence.

Angie had been a very popular person in her village, so I suggested that there would be people who would like to pay tribute to her, and we could have a service of Thanksgiving at the end of February. This happened. It was a wonderful celebration, with her daughter playing in a wind quartet with her school friends, a group from the choir which Angie, another sister and I had belonged to, our choir master playing the organ for hymns and my sisters and I giving a tribute. We had a retiring offering for the charity Cancer Research and finished the afternoon in the village hall for refreshments while looking at photographs of family life. It was an occasion at which her teenage daughter and her cousins could participate.

Children brought up in a Christian environment think about the 'hereafter' and the possibility of heaven. Cynthia asked, 'When you go to heaven are you still the same person you were? If you had a limp do you still have one in Heaven or do you become new?' Here is a 'concrete' thinker puzzling about the hereafter and questioning if it is like our experience of living today on earth.

John is a ten-year-old on the autism spectrum. One day on the way home from school, the children with their mothers walked quickly past a dead cat in the road, horrified. John stopped, was very emotional and asked his mother, 'What can we do?' As one of a Roman Catholic family, his mother suggested saying a prayer. With no inhibitions John said a prayer aloud and then said to his mother, 'It's OK now; the cat is with Jesus in heaven' and walked on with determination. Here is the assurance of faith.

In the New Testament, there is a saying when Jesus refers to an incident in the market place which he must have observed (Luke 7.32). He noticed children playing at funerals. What was happening? Perhaps like children today they were replaying something that they had experienced in order to make sense of it.

A colleague, George, took the funeral of the child of one of his church leaders. The child had been killed by a reversing dustcart which had not noticed him. He wept when he saw the small coffin and continued to cry as he took the funeral. Later in the day he went to the parents and apologised. The parents said that it was the most helpful thing that had happened. This was a shared grief.

Scholars cite the story of Jesus at the death of his friend Lazarus (John 11), when Jesus wept. There is a conversation with Mary, Lazarus's sister, about the resurrection. Jesus calls out to Lazarus, who is buried in a stone sepulchre, 'Come forth'. When Lazarus appears bound in the grave clothes, Jesus says, 'Unbind him, set him free.' Scholars wonder if the story is a parable of Jesus' own burial and resurrection, although knowledge of the raising of Lazarus is one of the reasons that the Jewish leaders gave for wanting the death of Jesus as a trouble maker. At the last meal he had with his friends he said, 'Do this is in remembrance of me.' Christians believe that although it is right to grieve at funerals, death is not the end since there is a life to come.

The adolescent motorbikers whose experience began this chapter contributed to the funeral by keeping a vigil for their friends who had died. On the whole adolescent lads and young men personify the saying, 'boys don't cry'. There is evidence that the emotional development of men is deficient: 'No matter how modern a society we have become and how diverse a society we have become, we still seem to educate our children in a feeling that they have to "man up", that they have to be strong, that they can't talk about emotions' (Moore 2015). Emotional education of young men and boys is needed (see Cohen 2001). A funeral such as this one can give a priest the opportunity to talk to adolescents and for them to ask questions: 'Why did it happen? Is there a God? Will they meet their friends in heaven? Is it a problem that they will be so much older than the deceased friend?'

> For the funerals of young people many bereaved families now ask for a small 'private' service, followed by a large memorial service. But seeing the coffin at the funeral is really important for young friends; so try to allow as many to come as want to. (*Church Times* 2014)

Dr Tess Kuin Lawton, Chaplain of Magdalen College School, Oxford goes on to say:

> If one has counselled the parents of a young person who has died the temptation is to plan the service from the family's perspective of the teenagers, which – theologically speaking – focuses on the crucifixion.

If we see the funeral from the perspective of the teenagers, however, an emphasis on pain simply leads to the response 'We can go out and do whatever we want in life, and live it large, because tomorrow may never come...' Instead, why not tackle the short life of the young teenager directly and reflect on the gifts of the Holy Spirit which the person brought to those who knew him or her? Give those who are left a blueprint for life now, and try and give a sense that, whatever the span of days we have, we have the opportunity to be someone wonderful. (*Church Times* 2014)

When the motorcyclists were killed many of the adults were left feeling helpless. Teenagers are probably able to cope better, since they are used to the emotional chaos of adolescence and use Facebook and other social media to share memories and photos of those who have died, thus grieving in an active way.

Islam

Families who are second and third generation settlers in Britain may continue in the traditions of their forefathers in 'rites of passage' and desire the occasions of dying and death to observe strict practices. They may return the bodies of deceased loved ones to the country of 'origin'. Others have adapted and taken on British customs, while some have a mixture of practices. Whatever is the case it is important to be sensitive to the beliefs and rites of others.

In Islam, those surrounding dying person encourage him to say the '*shahada*' confirming that there is no God but Allah. At death, those present say '*Inna lllahi wa inna ilayhi raji'un*': 'Verily, we belong to Allah, and truly to Him shall we return.' In Islamic law the body should be buried as soon as possible from the time of death, ideally within 24 hours, a custom that is probably rooted in an age when there was no refrigeration and no way of keeping the body for long without it decomposing.

Funeral prayers are said by all members of the community including children, though in a prayer or study room or the mosque's courtyard, not in the mosque itself, facing Mecca in three lines with the male most closely related to the deceased in the first line, followed by men, then children and then women. After prayers, the body is transported to the cemetery for burial. Traditionally only men are allowed to be present, though in some communities women will be allowed at the graveside. The grave is dug perpendicular to Mecca (the *qiblah*) and the body placed in the grave on its right side, facing the *qiblah*, while those so doing recite, 'In the name of Allah and in the faith of the Messenger of Allah.' Once in the grave a layer of wood or stones should be placed on top of the body to prevent direct contact with the soil that will fill the grave. Then each mourner places three handfuls of earth into the grave. Once filled a small stone or marker is placed at the grave, so that is it recognisable. Traditionally, it is prohibited to erect a large monument on the grave or decorate the grave in an elaborate way. After the funeral, the immediate family gathers to receive visitors. The community provide food for the mourning family for the first three days of mourning. In Islam, it is acceptable to express grief, crying and weeping over a death and at the funeral, but not wailing or shrieking which may express a lack of faith in Allah.

Hinduism

A Hindu funeral is a remembrance and a celebration service. Traditionally, the deceased is cremated on the *ghats* in Varanasi on the shores of the River Ganges. The body is no longer needed; it is the soul, the inner self, that is significant. White is the traditional colour for funerals together with traditional Indian garments. The chief mourner, usually the eldest son, and the other male members of the family may shave their heads as a mark of respect. This son lights the funeral pyre. Sound is part of the ritual with the ringing of bells. If the service is in the UK, where outdoor cremations are not allowed, the eldest son will press the button to make the coffin disappear and sometimes be allowed to ignite the cremator. Sometimes, the ashes are taken back to India to be scattered in the Ganges, though in some areas where there is a large community of Hindus, areas of water have been considered as acceptable substitutes. Mourning lasts for between two and five weeks.

Buddhism

Buddhism emphasises impermanence: the cycle of birth, death and rebirth. The Buddha recognised that the impermanence resulting from suffering characterised human life; only by the loss of attachment to the self through a series of rebirths could enlightenment and freedom be found. Theravada Buddhists believe in instant reincarnation; *The Book of Death* proposes that the art of living well and the art of dying well are one and the same. Acceptance is a good thing, taught Buddhists, for it will be followed by rebirth in an endless cycle until you can break free. It also provides an opportunity to assist the deceased as she fares on to the new existence. In Buddhism, death marks the transition from this life to a new mode of existence within the round of rebirths. For the living, death is a powerful reminder of the Buddha's teaching on impermanence.

> When Death in all its ferocity has arrived on the scene no bargaining can ward him off, no gifts, no attempt at sowing dissension, no force of arms and no restraint. Our hold on life on life is so uncertain that it is not worth relying on… Who, unless he be quite mad would make plans which do not reckon with death, when he sees the world so unsubstantial and frail like a water bubble? (Conze 1959)

Tantric Buddhists believe in an intermediate *bardo* period, as much as 49 days between death and rebirth. Tibetan monks guide the deceased's spirit through the perilous bardo by reading from the *Book of the Dead*. The bardo is divided into three phases. During the first it is in a swoon, constantly urged to enter the clear light of ultimate reality and recognise its own Buddha status. During the second the soul recovers and becomes aware and frightened by its own disembodied identity. It gradually becomes aware that it has died and sees the dismantling of its life. Finally it enters the 'illusory mental body' of a child, a dream-like state. The body is carried out in a sedan chair for cremation accompanied by monks, musicians, relatives and friends. Fire is considered to burn away attachments as well as sins. Clothes and personal possessions are then auctioned. Meanwhile the soul in bardo is buffeted, then judged. Six weeks after death the *bardo* may still be buffeted. It may overcome its egoistic goals and overcomes egocentricity becoming part of the ceaseless flow of life. It may enter a woman at intercourse and be re-born.

Drawing together experience and cultural context leading to practical implications

The funeral is a rite of passage, a significant event, usually arranged by the family of the deceased or, if there is no family, by the local authority. This is considered a moral obligation to a fellow human being. 'Funerals are important since they mark the passing of a human being from the society of the living to the world of the dead. Death is a passage which the funeral formalises' (Sheppy 2003, p.78). Ewan Kelly, a hospital chaplain and university lecturer, recalls the following incident:

> Several years ago in a large housing estate in Craigmillar, Edinburgh, a new born baby was found dead and abandoned on some waste ground. Neither the baby's mother nor father was ever traced. However, the whole community took ownership of the baby and rallied round to pay for the funeral, which the local minster performed and many attended. A unique human being had lived, albeit briefly, and died who needed to be respectfully laid to rest in a culturally appropriate way. (Kelly 2008, p.74)

The ritual was the responsibility of the local authority, but a community hearing the story were touched by it and wanted the baby to be recognised and ministered to by people who cared.

Often children are not consulted about seeing the body, visiting the Chapel of Rest or attending the funeral. Decisions are made for them. Is this protecting children from death, which continues to be deemed unsuitable for children? A way of thinking that sees children as innocent of suffering and death, not thinking about asking children and adolescents or giving them the information they might need so that the youngsters can make a reasoned choice. We need to listen to children to find out what they do understand and know. Is it an unnecessary cocooning of children if we don't? One eleven-year-old on the cusp of adolescence said, 'Adults don't help when they don't listen to children's opinions. They make decisions for them when they don't know' (Cranwell 2007; Wordern 1996). Overprotection from the realities of life, such as suffering and death, leads to a child lacking self-confidence when dealing with adversity and a consequent loss of self-esteem.

ACTIVITIES TO ELICIT THE READER'S EXPERIENCE

1. Look at a funeral service sheet, or jot one down from memory. This should be a funeral at which children were present. How were the children related to the deceased? What part did children play in the service? Describe what happened to make children feel part of the service.

2. Prepare a questionnaire on children/adolescent's attendance at a funeral. For example:

    *   What age were they when they attended?

    *   Whose funeral was it?

    *   Where did the funeral happen?

    *   Did they know what would happen at the funeral?

    *   Did anyone prepare them for the occasion?

    *   Did they meet the celebrant before the service?

    *   Were they asked if they wanted to take part?

    *   Did any children/ adolescents take part?

    *   What surprised them about the occasion?

    *   What were their feelings on the occasion?

Ask a local school if in an RE lesson on rituals such as funerals the questionnaire could be completed. Write up your findings.

7

Continuing Care of Children and Adolescents

Do kids get to stay with other kids or do they have to stay with grown-ups?

(Jackson in Marshall 2003, p.34)

A child's experience

Jamie was one of twins. At a year old, he and his twin sister had contracted meningitis. It was treated, but his sister sadly died. Each week, he was taken by his mother to the cemetery to visit his sister's grave. This seemed to him to be a feature of the week and as a small child he accepted it as normal. Later as an adolescent talking to his chums, he realised it was not normal to visit the cemetery as a child.

None of his chums had such a memory. In fact, they were rather dismissive of any talk about death. It was 'emotional girls' stuff'. Jamie was getting to the stage when he wanted more independence from his family and in particular his mother, so he refused to continue going with her, which caused a rift between them. Now in his late 60s, he still mentions the death of his twin when any discussion turns to the subject of death, perhaps because he was never able to grieve in a way appropriate to his age as a child.

Reflection on experience

Was his mother right to take Jamie to the cemetery? She needed to express her own grief and visiting was one way of grieving, but should she have made some other arrangements for the care of her young son while she did this? Are we right as adults to extend, or impose, our feelings and actions on a child? Grief is not limited to adults; Jamie himself needed to grieve for a twin sister whom he had spent the first year of his life with and was his companion and playmate; he must have missed her and questioned her absence. It would seem that at the time when his sister died, more than 60 years ago, the grief of children was not recognised.

An adolescent's experience

Rosie was an only child. Her mum had died some three years previously of a brain tumour. Rosie was the top scholar in the public exam results in her school and had to get her results from the head teacher himself. He said how proud her mother would have been at her success. One day she woke to the cries of her cat Mouser. Her back legs were paralysed, and she was in obvious pain. Her father was away for the weekend, so Rosie had to make decisions. Although it was a Sunday, she rang her friend, and together they managed to get an emergency appointment at the vets, taking the cat in her basket. The vet stated that Mouser could be operated on, but the outcome was uncertain. Rosie decided that it was better if Mouser was made pain-free through being put to sleep while she held her. Later, with her friend, she took Mouser's body home, and they buried Mouser under her favourite apple tree in the garden. That evening she rang her aunt who lived nearby and went to see her. She recounted the events of the morning then suddenly burst into uncontrollable sobbing.

Reflection on experience

Mouser had been a part of Rosie's life since childhood. She and her mum had bought Mouser together as a rescue cat. Now Mouser had died and another tie with her mother had been broken. Her aunt let her sob and simply held her tightly and stroked her hair. An adolescent's grief at the death of a parent is long lasting, particularly for a girl when her mother dies. Grief floods in as waves. Sometimes there is no obvious reason for the resurgence of grief. Often there is a trigger which is part of the story of the adolescent and the relationship with the deceased. In Rosie's experience, it was another death, this time of a cat, but a cat that held very precious memories for part of her life and her late mother's for many years. Mouser's death brought back all the memories of a happy childhood with her cat and her mum. Now both were gone.

Linking adult, child and adolescent experience

There is no set pattern or time limit to grief for a child or adolescent. Much depends on such factors as the personality of the bereaved, for example the attitude and acceptance, or not, of loss; the relationship of the bereaved with the deceased; and the nature of the death, whether anticipated through lengthy illness or unexpected. Each of these factors has been mentioned in earlier chapters. Grieving never ends; it is something that we never get over if the relationship has been loving and significant. The Dougy Center comments, 'This is perhaps one of the least understood aspects of grief in our society' (The Dougy Center 2006, p.7). A death of someone close to you leaves a vacuum in your life, and life is never the same again. Many adults, however, seem to want to put the loss behind them and get on with life, but a loss does not mean that they will never be happy and joyous again. The experience of loss can be transformed into something positive. Draper called the process of transformation 're-imaging': thinking about the future and the bereaved so that adult, child or adolescent can carry the deceased person with him into his future in a new way (Draper 2008, p.7). The sociologist Tony Walter suggested an integration: the bereaved carrying with him the deceased, since the latter was part of his present life story (Walter 1990).

Sociological, psychological and historical insights

Children are different from adults in their approach to death. They are much more resilient; even young children losing a parent sometimes adjust if there is another care-giver who is able to fulfil the needs of the child. Slightly older children oscillate between sadness and getting on with life, but that tends not to last long: life is for living. Adolescents grieve at the death of someone close to them, and if they are truthfully told about the death and involved in the funeral arrangements, they find support amongst their peer group and eventually move on and continue in the establishing of their own identity. However, grief re-emerges at certain milestones in the lives of children and adolescents, since grief does not have a particular end time.

There is little understanding that a child and adolescent will need to revisit a bereavement, particularly if the death of a parent happened at an early point in his life. And as the years pass the bereaved child, now a young adult, wants to know more about the death, remember it and share memories of the lost loved one. When the surviving parent cooperates with anecdotes and memories that the child has forgotten, it enriches both parent and young person and adds to the quality of their relationship. These occasions can be 'rubbished' and denied their significance by others, particularly if as a child there was counselling and returning can be dismissed as morbid curiosity. However, those early memories are part of a life story. I remember that when eventually my niece Rosie had a steady boyfriend who had never known Rosie's late mother, I brought out some photos of Rosie as a child and some of the drawings she had done for me and how delighted Rosie was, wanting to know more about them.

Rosie, as she becomes a young adult, will have occasions of significance such as gaining a place at university, later graduating, getting a first job, perhaps getting married. These are occasions when Rosie will reach a new development level as a person or experience a personal accomplishment which her mother would be proud of, but will not be there to share, and she is likely to re-connect and grieve for her mother's death. This means that the care of children and adolescents must be ongoing, so that each has the resources to live into a positive adulthood.

In Chapter 4, we saw how a young family could prepare for the ultimate death of a terminally ill parent. The preparation was twofold. First, it was noticing the changes in the health of the sick parent, and second, it was changing behaviour in response to the observations. The family were then able to anticipate the death and begin the process of building positive memories to carry the person with them after the death. For some when the death is unexpected this process is unlikely to be possible and with an imminent death a child may be angry or sad, which may well be expressed in unusual behaviour at home and in school. Such emotions as anger may arise after the funeral when the finality of the death is realised. Anger wells up inside and bursts out. Other children may be silent and withdrawn. The ongoing welfare of the child or adolescent is then paramount. This continues to be a grieving process, until someone is found to whom they can talk openly and honestly. It may involve a parent or a teacher in school listening to help a child or adolescent face what has happened and begin to accept the normality and finality of death and so move on. The recognition of the significance of grief in developed societies, however, is counter-cultural in the light of adult reluctance to talk about death.

The public recognition of grief and the culture that surrounds it, both in public and in private, has changed over the last century and a half. A major factor was the death of Queen Victoria's husband Albert who died at 43 after 21 years of marriage. Queen Victoria was a widow for 40 years and wore black for 40 years, setting the tone of an obsessive celebration of grief for her subjects. The First and Second World Wars influenced attitudes to grief with the high death rates of soldiers. The historian Jalland notes that the Second World War 'marked a deeper break with the past than the Great War and the process was cumulative. A pervasive model of silence about death and of suppressed grieving became entrenched in the English psyche' (Jalland 2013, p.63). Churchill called for courage and stoicism during the blitz of British cities: 'The dark side of the blitz story was sanitized to sustain morale' (p.63). Public grief was discouraged; grief was privatised and despised. The thinking was to 'keep busy and pretend to be cheerful' and to grieve in private and in silence. Women imitated men in suppressing grief. Subsequently, the atrocities of the Holocaust shook people's faith in humanity. It seemed a prostitution of the advances of contemporary medical science, bringing disbelief. Nuclear proliferation became a fear. Thoughts about death were further marginalised with the Welfare State provision of pension rights and sick leave, relieving some of the financial distress of bereavement; medical advances resulted in longer life and in death becoming more remote.

The importance of parents and other professionals recognising the continuing needs of children and adolescents is significant. For example, in schools in the UK increasingly there is a policy which recognises the long-term effects of bereavement in regard to the behaviour of pupils with the school having access to outside support services if bereavement issues persist and appear to becoming 'pathological'.

Following the Harvard Child Bereavement Study in the late 1980s, Dr J William Worden, one of the study's directors, was interviewed. Worden found that about 20 per cent of children who were grieving needed intervention two years after their bereavement, contrasting with the control group which was closer to 9–11 per cent. One variable that strongly affected the functioning of a child was the functionality of the surviving parent, a depressed parent, not being able to consistently maintain homework and discipline, which resulted in a child having a more difficult time adjusting to the loss (Hospice Foundation of America 1990).

What are some more subtle warning signs that a young person is struggling and needs more help? One significant concern is when a child exhibits significant sudden changes in behaviour. Of course, short-term changes may be normal but if the changes are persistent or striking – for example, the usually social child doesn't want to be around anyone – this may be a cause of concern. A few 'red flag' signs that may indicate the need for further assessment by a mental health professional are, first, a child who cannot speak about the dead person, or leaves the room when the person's name is mentioned; second, a child whose aggression becomes destructive, especially if this is new or unusual behaviour; third, a child who when a parent dies develops persistent and increasing anxiety about the surviving parent, which may develop into phobic behaviour about not leaving that parent to go to school.

It is important to look at these in the context of the death; many of these behaviours may be typical soon after the death, but if they continue they may be more serious. In any of these situations, it is important for teachers to take the time to listen well, to be patient and to develop relationships in which a level of trust is increasing with the children they work with, so they can offer them the best support through this challenging time. The focus should not be on the presence of a symptom or behaviour but on its duration. If any of these behaviours continue for several months, it is likely that professional help is needed. Symptoms are prolonged bodily distress, sleep disturbance, persistent changes in eating patterns, aggressive behaviour, marked social withdrawal, school difficulties or serious academic reversal, persistent self-blame or guilt, self-destructive behaviour or expressing a desire to die. Young people report very different experiences at school. 'But it is known that how the school manages the individual is critical. Teachers make a real difference' (see the Grief Encounter entry in the Useful Websites and Organisations section).

Believers' experiences – world faiths

For all who have lost a child or adolescent, there is a worldwide candle lighting ceremony on the second Sunday of December every year starting at 7.00pm in each time zone. This was initiated by The Compassionate Friends in the USA as their gift to grieving families. This candle lighting ceremony unites friends and families in loving memory of all children who have died at any age from any cause, transcending all boundaries of global grieving communities.

Within children's hospices there are regular times when the grief and continuing care of siblings of children who have died are recognised. Some hospices, for example, organise balloon decorating with the name of the deceased child written on an attached tag so that siblings can release the balloons, which fly away, symbolically carrying the loved one with them. Such ritual occasions are important for children and adolescents.

Judaism

Within Judaism there are continuing ceremonies when a child and adolescent can remember and continue to be in touch with a deceased parent or grandparent. One such occasion is when the headstone of the grave is erected a year after the death at *Yahrzeit*. The headstone, *Matzava*, can be as elaborate or simple as the family wishes. Most often the person's Hebrew name is inscribed on the headstone along with the dates of birth and death. There is often a ceremony around this event. Annually at the anniversary of a death sons recite the *Kaddish* for a parent, parents for a child in the synagogue, and all mourners light a candle in honour of the deceased that burns for 24 hours, while close relatives recite the mourner's prayer, 'May He remember...' Visitors to those mourning should not offer platitudes but encourage grief to be expressed.

On the annual Jewish festivals of *Yom Kippur, Shemini Atzeret* and *Shavu'ot* those who have died are remembered. *Yom Kippur* is the Day of Atonement with acts of confession and a time of repentance (*teshuva*) leading to healing, for example confessing guilt over the lack of care given to a loved one. Children may think that they were guilty of a death when a child was angry with a parent and wished the parent was dead, particularly when the parent was later involved in a fatal traffic accident. At the festivals of *Shemini Atzeret*, the last day of Passover and *Shavu'ot* all relatives recite the mourner's prayer. Grief is honoured and taken up into remembrance of a loved one. Mourners placing pebbles on graves is an increasingly popular custom. It is likely to have pagan origins but has come to symbolise the permanence of memory of the deceased and is honoured by children and young people.

Christianity

Within Christianity grief is recognised as significant, though it is balanced by hope of an afterlife when Christians believe that they will meet God and their loved ones again. The young boy Jackson's concern quoted at the beginning of the chapter – 'Do kids get to stay with other kids or do they have to stay with grown-ups?' – indicates the belief in an afterlife, and speculates what it will be like (Marshall 2003, p.34).

At particular times in the Christian year those who have died are remembered and these occasions are a recognition of the deceased and for children and adolescents are implicitly examples of continuing care for those who have lost a close family member. Christmas can be a time when families notice an empty chair and remember and comfort one another on the loss of a loved one. At our family Christmas occasions we always have a toast to 'absent friends' and the significance of this is remembering those younger members of the family who have 'flown the nest' and are now living abroad; and also those of the family who have 'passed beyond us': our parents and in particular our sister, Angie.

At the beginning of Lent the service of Ash Wednesday reminds Christians of their mortality, as a cross of ashes is made on the head of those attending and the following words spoken: 'God, our Father, you create us from the dust of the earth, grant that these ashes may be a sign of our penitence and a symbol of our mortality', and later, 'Remember that you are dust and to dust you shall return.' Lent culminates in the events of Easter. At Easter, Christians remember the events of the passion of Jesus: the crucifixion on Good Friday, followed by the death of Jesus and his burial in the rock tomb. On Holy Saturday, Christians remember the desolation of those first Christians at Jesus' death. This becomes for some a remembering of the parting from loved ones.

On one occasion, I was asked to visit two children who were desolate because their beloved grandfather had died on Holy Saturday and they thought that Jesus was dead in the tomb and so not in heaven to welcome their grandfather. Together we discovered that Jesus' death happened a long time ago, but Christians believe that something happened subsequently, the mystery called the Resurrection. The Spirit of Jesus was freed and his presence is with us today so would be in heaven to welcome the children's grandfather. This was an occasion when these two children needed continuing care after a bereavement.

On Easter Day, in some churches, the names of those who have died during the previous year are read aloud at some point during the services, bringing comfort to the bereaved, adults and children alike.

The dead are also remembered at the celebration of All Souls. This occurs on 2 November and has become mixed up with Halloween. Halloween probably evolved from the Celts 2000 years ago with their pagan priests, the Druids. The most significant festival of the Druids was Samhain, the Druid New Year, celebrating the end (or death) of the summer and its fruitfulness. The festival began on 31 October and lasted three days until 2 November. Samhain was the festival of the dead, and it was believed at this time that the spirits of the dead were very close and visited the living. Today at Halloween, children, dressed up as skeletons and ghosts, 'trick or treat' when an idle threat is made to perform mischief and a gift of food given as a reward.

Since the eighth century, in the British Isles, Christians celebrated All Saints (All Hallows) to coincide with or replace the Celtic festival of Samhain. All Saints Day on 1 November celebrated all saints – the ones officially recognised by the Church and the many unknown ones. This was followed by All Souls beginning at vespers on All Hallows.

All Souls Day is dominated by the sense of human mortality and is centred on penitence and intercession. It is linked with the funeral liturgy and many churches have latterly used All Souls to help the recently bereaved. A service of comfort for grief is held and can be accessed by children as part of their continuing care. Many churches offer the opportunity to light candles for loved ones who have died. The names of the deceased are read out during the service.

A few days later, the parade and service at the Cenotaph is held in London, and around war memorials throughout the UK, to remember those who have died in the World Wars. Young uniformed organisations take part in these occasions. Again in the parades children participate since some have lost a father in war and it must be a source of comfort to them to be surrounded by others who are acknowledging and honouring those who have died in war. A recent remembering was the installation at the Tower of London, 'Blood Swept Lands and Seas of Red', marking the centenary of the outbreak of the First World War, where the artists Paul Cummins and Tom Piper made 888,246 ceramic poppies. Thousands visited the Tower between July and November 2014. An exhibition of the poppies is now on tour of UK. Not only did visitors with families remember losses in the past of the World Wars, but it evoked in them memories of their own losses.

On the continent, in Roman Catholic countries, there are annual occasions for the bereaved to remember their loved ones. In Spain, families gather and eat roasted chestnuts and almond cakes, a remnant of the custom of leaving offerings with the bodies of the dead. In France, chrysanthemums decorate the graves of the departed. In Poland, families take flowers, candles and even picnics with them to the cemeteries where their relatives are buried. Mexicans celebrate 'The Day of the Dead' in honour of their ancestors. The Spanish conquerors of Mexico moved the event to All Saints Day and All Souls Day, the first and second of November. The festival honours and remembers loved ones who have died, believing that the souls of the deceased return each year to visit the living. On All Saints Day, children are remembered and their gravestones are decorated with toys and balloons. All Souls Day remembers deceased adults; they are honoured by the building of altars, lovingly decorated with flowers, candles and photos. Family members gather at the gravesides and have picnics, serving the favourite foods of the deceased; they tell stories and remember the times they shared with their loved ones. The ritual is rooted in pride. The family want to create the most welcoming homecoming for their loved one and to reassure them they will never be forgotten. These customs and rituals are an indication of the ongoing remembrance of the beloved departed and are on taking the deceased with us and recognising their significance in the present to families, including children.

Some churches also offer services on Holy Innocents Day, 28 December, specifically for those who have lost children either through death or miscarriage.

Islam

There is some debate about whether or not the dead are remembered. The period of mourning lasts for 40 days after the death. After this period, scholars believe that with current knowledge of mourning, to continue simply reactivates grief, so is unnecessary. However, there is a belief that the dead may pray and comfort the living.

Hinduism

Hindus traditionally remember their dead with a yearly ritual known as the *shraddha* ceremony. *Shraddha*, coming from a word meaning 'faith', is performed annually on the date of a Hindu's death. It is tradition to first conduct the rites in the days immediately after a death in order to help the individual's soul move onto their next reincarnation. Death rites are important, not only for the future of the deceased, but also for the continued comfort and welfare of the living. Immediately after a death, the individual's soul is believed to linger around its living family and may cause them harm until the *shraddha* rites are performed, letting the soul move to its next reincarnated life. In the days immediately after death, families gather for a large meal to celebrate the deceased. They generally offer rice balls (*pinda*) to the dead family member, who is represented by a photograph. Then a Hindu priest offers four rice balls: one large representing the recently deceased, the other three small representing the preceding generations awaiting reincarnation. The large ball is split and combined with the smaller pieces symbolising how the deceased is reunited with their ancestors. The ball is then fed to a cow.

The annual *shraddha* service in remembrance of the deceased is similar to the rites conducted immediately after death. Family members often bring a priest into the home in order to make a *pinda* offering

to both the recently deceased and other close ancestors. The offerings
are food for the soul which has undergone the many ceremonies after
death. The yearly memorial service is generally performed as long as
the sons of the deceased are still living. The service of Hindu death
rituals is traditionally conducted by men, a difficulty if there are no
sons. When the annual *shraddha* is conducted, it is common for the
son only to mention the names of males in his family's ancestral lines
when making an offering. In some Hindu beliefs, a deceased woman
is said to merge with her male ancestors, thus including women in the
service.

Buddhism

Some Buddhists believe that a link with dead loved ones can be made,
though others are more skeptical. The link is through a medium; the
experience brings comfort and a continuing relationship with the
deceased.

Care is also evidenced in Mahayana Buddhism's thinking of
bodhisattvas, a person with serenity, acceptance of things as they are,
and loving. A Zen Buddhist said, 'In all its dimension, and all its variety,
I see…a quality in someone. In the last place that you're looking
for it…you see more *bodhisattva* activities, more holy activities…in
supermarkets than in churches or temples' (Bowker 1983, p.262;
Brown 1975), these are forms of continuity and care when those on
the edge of *nirvana* turn back in order to help others still on the way.

Drawing together experience and cultural context leading to practical implications

It has been noted in this chapter that many children are resilient
and if given time and preparation for the death of someone close to
them, such as a parent or a favourite grandparent, grieve well. Later at
adolescence when they reach a new development level as a person or
experience a personal accomplishment, they often feel the absence of
a birth parent keenly. This may occur in reaching the age of majority,
18 years in the UK, or at a time of personal accomplishment such as
success in public examinations, winning a university place, gaining a
degree or starting their first job. In some ways, the grieving process
never stops, unless we are able to carry memories of the loved one with

us always. This means being able to talk about those memories, the challenging ones and the joyful ones, freely and openly with family and friends.

In the early months and years following a bereavement both a child and an adolescent are likely to need continuing care. This care needs to be tailored to him at a time when he needs help. With younger children it is ideal if the surviving parent works with them so that they can talk about their respective griefs, which can be very helpful to the child. There are activities that can be suggested and objects that can be made which will help the process of bereavement and sustain a child. With older children and adolescents the task can be chosen by them and they can proceed with it alone, though with encouragement through progress to completion.

There are a range of tasks which can be attempted. Some of the following are from my personal experience and some from other sources. A selection of published resources is included in the Further Reading section at the end of the book. Some of the tasks need materials which are easily accessible; others will need to be purchased.

Practical things to do

The following are some suggestions of things to do with, or be done by, a child or adolescent to remember a deceased parent, grandparent or sibling – someone who has been close to him and whose absence continues to grieve him.

A memory box

This involves an old shoe box in reasonable condition, which many shoe shops will give to you if you ask. This can be decorated with scraps of paper in the colour that the deceased liked or covered in handprints in bright poster paint. It can be filled with reminders of the person, for example someone's favourite earrings, the remains of a bottle of perfume, photos. For a male, reminders could be a cufflink, a tie, one of the cigarettes left, part of his daily newspaper and photos. The memory box could be added to, with poems written about the person by the child or adolescent and a story using one of the memories of the person. It might be kept in a special place on completion and be brought out at the birthday of the deceased, or the anniversary of the death, or a family occasion such as Christmas. Winston's Wish has a free activity sheet on making a memory box and 'readymade' boxes for sale (see the Useful Websites and Organisations section).

A memory garden

One of my sisters was able to buy a two metre-wide extension to her small garden which backs on to a local landowner's property. She calls it Angie's garden in memory of our sister. There are cultivated flowers and shrubs that my sister enjoyed and it is a living memory to her. Any child or adolescent can use a part of their garden as a memory garden, or even a large plant pot, choosing what is to be planted or set in the garden and cultivating it. It could be a place for quiet reflection. Another idea is to set aside and cultivate a window box.

A family tree

If the deceased is a relative, a family tree could be made on the pinboard in the kitchen where everyone can see it. Children will need help with this; adolescents might need advice with names. Talking together and finding photos to match the names are part of the activity. This is part of the process to incorporate the living and the dead, and to continue to support a bereaved child.

Anagrams

This task is from The Dougy Center (2006). Paper and pens will be needed for this task to 'remember and memorialise the person who died' (p.31), and is suitable for seven- to ten-year-olds. The child or adolescent writes the name of the person who died vertically on a piece of paper, a letter per line. Then invite him to write down words, sentences and phrases which 'remind them of the person, using the letters of the name' (p.31). Following the task his remembrances can be shared.

A First Aid kit

This activity is adapted from *Muddles, Puddles and Sunshine: Your Activity Book to Help When Someone Has Died* (Crossley 2000, p.25). Use an old shoe box or plastic container and pieces of paper and a pen. The child can decorate the box as a First Aid kit. Then on each piece of paper he can write down something you would find in a First Aid kit. He should then use other pieces of paper and draw a border around each piece (this distinguishes each set). On the second set of paper with the borders, he can write down or draw a First Aid kit for a bad day, that is, a day when grief is hard: for example, phone up and talk to a friend. The child can share what he has written with an adult. You can buy 'A Pocket Full of Plasters' online from Winston's Wish (see the Useful Websites and Organisations section). It contains ten 'plasters' the size of a credit card which can be put in a pocket and brought out by a young person when he is hurting from a bereavement.

A book of thoughts

This activity is adapted from The Dougy Center (2006). You will need some A4 paper (or if possible A3) folded in half and stapled to make a booklet. The goal is 'to facilitate journal writing as a way of processing grief' (p.32). Write a question or topic at the top of some of the pages; other pages might be left blank for whatever the person is feeling. Headings might include: memory, colours, emailing, favourite things, holidays and food. Each page should be illustrated with a story, poem or drawing about what the child or adolescent is thinking and feeling at present. The exercise could also be done about the deceased. Later the child or adolescent can share whatever is desired with an adult, parent or teacher. An extension of this idea is found in the 'From You to Me Journals' produced by Winston's Wish. These are beautifully produced books which have around 60 questions carefully designed to inspire someone to tell a personal story. There are books for Mum, Dad, grandparent and friend. A possible use would be when a close relative is known to have a terminal illness or for someone who is old and reaching the end of their life, so that when that person dies the child or adolescent has a treasured memory to read and bring comfort to them.

Anniversary

On the anniversary of the death or the first birthday, think of an activity the deceased liked and spend the day doing this, for example going to the park and having a swing. If the weather is suitable you could take a picnic of the deceased's favourite food, or visit the seaside and sit on the seawall eating fish and chips.

Christmas tree decoration

Each year make a new tree decoration; this could be made from drinking straws, pieces of real straw, or out of card or playdough.

It could be in the shape of a star, a Christmas tree, a reindeer, an angel, or anything the child would like to make. Winston's Wish has a product called 'Wish upon a star: Wishing Stars' to write on messages such as 'Dear Dad missing you love' (see the Useful Websites and Organisations section).

Winston's Wish also publish a book called *Out of the Blue – Making Memories Last When Someone Has Died* (Stokes 2006). The book has been written and designed for teenagers to offer support through bereavement using a range of activities which can be completed by a teenager on his own, or with a family member or a professional. The activities allow feelings to be worked at and safely explored.

Practical responses

If a child finds sleeping difficult, a CD playing soothing music can help. If he is afraid of the dark, then a night light can also help.

Play can be a good way to work through difficult feelings. This can be of many sorts, for example having a plastic box with dressing up clothes in it. If it does not cause distress to the partner of the deceased, it could include some of their jewellery, hats and clothes. An adult could join this activity and suggest a theme or the child could choose.

ACTIVITIES TO ELICIT THE READER'S EXPERIENCE

Think about and list the ways your experience as parent or professional makes you aware of and continues to support a child or an adolescent who has experienced a loss by death.

8

Care of the Carers Including Ourselves

A child's experience

I was using a walking stick with difficulty following surgery to my leg. It was Easter time, and since a family I was visiting were Christians, they talked about the Easter story of death and new life. Toby, a bright seven-year-old, was speculating about heaven and what it was like. Suddenly he blurted out to me, 'You won't need your walking stick when you die. The angels will carry you up to heaven.'

Reflection on experience

I felt that I was being cared for and was humbled by the experience. Children can be amazing in their sensitivity and in weighing up a situation and making connections. Toby did just that in seeing my stick and responding to my lack of mobility. The experience linked with Sarah's comment above, 'Dear God help me to learn from other people' (Durran 1985, p.61). I had misjudged Toby's ability to make connections between his life and his faith.

An adolescent's experience

After first teaching in a grammar school, since the local authority were moving to a comprehensive education scheme I thought that I must get experience with less able pupils and went to teach in a secondary modern school. One of my pupils was an attractive girl called Julie. Julie had a difficult home background with multiple 'fathers' coming and going. At the age of 15, she could barely read, but she loved needlework. Her behaviour was poor, sometimes outrageous, but I could only guess the reasons. She swore and stole, nothing was safe on my desk, yet somehow I felt that beneath Julie's bravado there was something to cultivate and given the chance, which she had never had, she could make something of her life. At that time is was possible in the UK to leave school at 15, and Julie was eager to do so. One of my tasks was to find jobs for these less able girls. I had contacts with a firm making high class ties, often a 'one-off' for a celebrity. I rang up my contact and asked if they would see Julie, mentioning her skills with a needle, but for my own benefit and others who I might send to this firm, I mentioned that Julie was 'light fingered'. Julie got the job, and before she left, came into my room and threw a bunch of wilting daffodils on my desk.

Two years later I was in the cinema queue when Julie came rushing up to me, to say that she was still in the same job, and the firm had opened a savings account for her.

Reflection on experience

Unexpected incidents happen in life, and the benefits are that as a professional sometimes you are cared for in a totally unexpected way. I suspected the wilting daffodils thrown on my desk at the end of term had been taken from the local church graveyard; nevertheless, they were a gesture of good will and showed Julie's caring, which was usually hidden. Julie's recognition of me, in a totally different environment from school, and her enthusiasm to come up to me of her own free will and talk was a wonderful experience. I felt that as a 'carer' I was cared for.

Linking adult, child and adolescent experience

Bereavement and grief are no respecters of persons or ages. When adults, children and adolescents suffer loss, each grieves but in a different way. Those of us who are parents and professionals, and who are given the responsibility of caring for children and adolescents as they work through the processes of loss and bereavement, have a challenging responsibility. It is an exhausting process working with children and trying to understand their thinking and behaviour and then discovering how help can be given in what is always a unique 'case', since each individual is different with varying circumstances and a life story to tell. The Dougy Center comments, 'Watching students cope with a death is a difficult and painful journey' (The Dougy Center 2006, p.19). The Dougy Center works within an education setting but the comments are equally appropriate for other professionals. The danger for the adult is 'burn-out'. Teachers from several schools cited the following factors as contributing to their stress:

- witnessing pain and distress experienced by the families
- feeling unskilled in dealing with emotional responses
- physical exhaustion as a result of emotional trauma
- poor communication between themselves and families or other carers.

(from Child Bereavement UK Information Pack Sheet 5: Looking after Yourself; see their website for details)

It is therefore important to form a strategy so that 'the carer can be cared for'. This is the context and subject of this chapter.

Sociological, psychological and historical insights

Recognising our own mortality and our losses

We all know that life itself is terminal! The one thing we all have in common is that one day we will die. Nevertheless, working with the bereaved can arouse strong emotional reactions within you, which may arise unexpectedly. We need to be prepared for this by being aware of our own attitudes to death, working through our own losses and coming to terms with, and facing, our own mortality. It happens some of these losses might well be ignited again by the grief of the children we work with (doing the 'Life Line' exercise which can be found at the end of this chapter will help: page 187). If, when working with a child or adolescent, a previous loss of your own surfaces and it feels too close to home, do not be afraid to give yourself a little time and space, perhaps saying something like, 'Let's simply be quiet for a few minutes, before we carry on.' This is not a sign of weakness; it merely recognises that we all have our human limitations. I remember as a hospital chaplain being called to be with a family who had lost a baby through a cot death. As they told me about their beloved baby Katie, something welled up within me which I tried to ignore so that I could concentrate on this family as they told their story. It was not until later that day that I had an opportunity to attend to my own emotions and realised that it could have been my niece of the same age and name that I was mourning. The resonance with our own experience or a personal connection with the person who has died must not come in the way of our care. It is an oft quoted truism to say, 'I know how you feel', but we can never know what another person is feeling. We can only walk alongside and listen.

In school, when a death occurs directly related to the classroom, it may be that of the relative of a pupil, a pupil or a member of staff, teaching or ancillary. It can activate memories of losses and deaths in teachers' own pasts. Many teachers feel that issues around bereavement are the responsibility of the home and not of the school, since this is a personal family occasion and not a public, school one. Other teachers feel that they do not like talking about death. However, because they are in a position of trust and outside the emotional whirlpool of the family, pupils may seek them out believing them to be a safe person to talk to. For these reasons, it is important that teachers work through their own agenda about death.

Training to support children and adolescents in bereavement issues

Many professionals such as teachers, youth workers, social workers and clergy, for whom bereavement was not their main training nor the focus of present work, may feel frustration at having to deal with difficult situations without adequate training to prepare them, a frustration which increases stress levels. Few have had the opportunity to learn about the way children and adolescents understand death or to explore the emotions and behaviour of children who have lost a loved one. There are several solutions to this.

In-service training

Teachers can ask the administration of the school/academy to include training sessions on dealing with bereaved children in their classrooms as an integral part of ongoing in-service training.

Bringing in specialists

These can come from a variety of different backgrounds such as a children's hospice doctor or senior nurse, a clinical psychologist or a Marie Curie nurse. It needs to be someone who works with children and adolescents and understands how these young people may react to bereavement and their concept development of death.

Books or online resources

There are an increasing number of books such as the classic text by J.W. Worden, *Children and Grief: When a Parent Dies* (1996) or more recently *Lost for Words: Loss and Bereavement Awareness Training* (Holland *et al.* 2005) and *Understanding Children's Experiences of Parental Bereavement* (Holland 2001).

Training courses

If you have a local hospice near you, enquire if they have bereavement counsellors you can consult or ask them to staff such a course for you. Those who are working daily in the context of death and dying have a wealth of 'hands on experience', informing and informed by their theoretical knowledge and their practice.

The knowledge of concept development on the subject of death will enable you to develop strategies to work with those seeking help. It also gives more confidence and reduces stress levels. In addition, it is important for teachers to look at where in the curriculum, as a normal routine, there are opportunities to deal with loss and death in the classroom so that it can be seen as a part of everyday life that each of us needs to face rather than something which is bolted on to another subject (see Chapter 5).

The task of a professional with a bereaved child or adolescent

Being alongside a child or adolescent in pain and distress can be very stressful, difficult and draining, but it is important to remember that 'the carer' (that is any professional to whom the child or adolescent turns) is not responsible for the child's grief and cannot carry it for her. The carer can listen and take in what she says, digest it and give it back to her. The imagery is of a cow digesting and chewing the cud! What the carer can offer is support on her journey through grief. We need to care, though with a certain level of detachment so that when silent and listening we do not feel guilty that we not doing enough. Professional boundaries must be remembered; we cannot carry grief for people but we can share their journey by being there. When the calm and the silence follow, we intuitively know that the mystery we call 'Love' or God is present in the situation.

Know your limitations

However hard the pain is, visible or not, and however great the need of the other person, do not over commit and offer something that is difficult to deliver.

It is helpful for the carer to know their own limitations, so do not offer more than you can deliver. It is better to offer something small but be constant in delivery than to go for the grand but unsustainable gestures. This will keep things manageable. For teachers, there should be a list of telephone numbers of other professionals such as psychologists and psychiatrists to whom the teacher can refer for advice, or suggest to the parents that more expert help is needed.

Be gentle with yourself

Remember your achievements – the simple gift you give to a bereaved child or adolescent might be giving a safe space to talk openly about all the difficult things that go through a child's head at a parental bereavement which cannot be talked about to a surviving parent, who is anyway too full of grief to hear what is being said. Listening is essential: being with a person rather than doing anything. You do not need to be an expert to provide effective advice and help, rather you need to be a mature adult who has lived through tough experience and knows that coming out of the tunnel is possible.

Grief issues take time to process, there is no set time frame

Remind yourself that you, the carer, are an enabler not a magician. We cannot change what has happened but we can be alongside a bereaved youngster in their journey. Be aware that this may be painful for you too, perhaps raising memories of your own losses. You as the carer are bound to feel helpless at times – admit to it without shame. However, distancing yourself protects you but can be perceived as not being supportive to an individual.

Self-knowledge

It is easy to be self-deluded about our own abilities. I cannot know myself completely. It is only as I reveal myself to another that I can know more of whom I am. Here the insight of the Johari Window conceived by Joseph Luft and Harrington Ingham (Luft and Ingham 1955) is helpful. I have adapted it in Figure 8.1.

1 'Free or public' area The part known to you and to others, the area of mutual sharing and interaction	**2 'Blind' area** Known to others, but you yourself are unaware of it It includes gestures, tone of voice, and good traits of which you are ignorant
3 'Hidden' area Known to you but not shared with others You might wish to keep some parts hidden	**4 'Unknown' area** An area where our creative talents and abilities as well as our fears and limitations lie, which we do not know about and others have never seen, yet a part of all of us

Figure 8.1 Adaptation of the Johari Window

1. *The Free or public area:* An aim is to enlarge this area.

2. *The Blind area:* You make this area smaller by getting feedback from others. Working with a group helps.

3. *The Hidden area:* It might help relationships if more of you were known and shared with colleagues with whom you are working. This can be done by self-disclosure.

4. *The Unknown area:* Meditation and relaxation may bring some of these feelings into awareness.

The more your 'Free self' coincides with your 'Whole self' and the more you share of yourself with the world, the better you communicate your true self to others and the less tension there is within yourself. There are ways to do this, for example by going to a counsellor and sometimes a mentor has the skills to help with this. This is about self-awareness and self-care.

Support groups

Each profession working with bereaved children and adolescents over difficult situations is likely to face exhaustion. We need to anticipate that we may experience an emotional reaction to a situation and realise that it is perfectly normal and OK to be emotionally affected. However, to help others we need to feel reasonably strong. Professionals acting as carers need a supportive management structure and specific colleagues to talk through any issues that concern them or which have a personal impact on them. Knowing the carer has a support network lightens the load and enables clearer thinking about action. There is a stress factor in 'holding material' told by a client in this sensitive area and within the bounds of confidentiality this could be shared.

Talk with others as the carer and trust in the support group about your feelings. Using a 'colleague' system regularly is a positive method of learning and growing as a professional. Within this group, as trust is developed between members of the group, you will be able to reflect on practice, for example where a colleague was uncertain of what to do or say, or uncertain of what they actually did. Sharing with other professionals, and knowing that others in your team are affected similarly when working with a depressed, bereaved child or a silent and tight adolescent, helps you to feel less alone and more able to care.

It is important to give one another feedback and support. Give encouragement to colleagues working with bereaved youngsters;

everyone needs this and it is important to accept it in return. Support others in the team. If you know someone in your team is going through a bad time, make time to ask after her or drop a card in her pigeonhole.

Many professionals today are required to have a mentor or a supervisor; the former is a trusted advisor and a supervisor refers to a person who observes and directs the work of an employee. These relationships built through regular meetings help, support and encourage self-help through discussion and create 'epiphany' moments, thereby raising professionalism in this difficult and challenging area of working with children and adolescents. There is a time factor in working with colleagues and having joint sharing and learning meetings in addition to individual supervision, but this is outweighed by the increase in professionalism, which benefits the young person.

Believers' experiences – world faiths

Judaism

On several occasions in the Hebrew Scriptures when individuals are 'stressed' in their anguish they are met by God. Jacob, fleeing from his brother Esau's threat to kill him, stops for rest (Genesis 27.41–3; 28.10–17). He dreams of a ladder stretching from earth to heaven, with angels ascending and descending and hears, 'Know that I am with you wherever you go, and will bring you back to this land: for I will not leave you until I have done what I have promised you' (Genesis 28.15). Years later Jacob decides to return home and be reconciled with his brother. Nearing home, fearful of the future meeting, he sends his household ahead (Genesis 32.22–4). Alone at the brook Jabbok, he wrestles with an unknown assailant (Genesis 28.24–30). At daybreak, Jacob discovers he has wrestled with God, One who is always present to bless. Rachel Naomi Remen, an oncologist, suggests a parallel with her own experience: 'Perhaps the wisdom lies in engaging the life you have been given as fully and courageously as possible and not letting go until you find the unknown blessing that is in everything' (Remen 2000, pp.25–7).

Elijah flees Queen Jezebel's anger and threat to kill him after his defeat of the prophets of Baal (1 Kings 18.20–40; 19.1–20). On his journey Elijah is fed and nourished. Finally, at Mount Horeb, after wind, earthquake and fire there is 'a sound of sheer silence' (v.12) –

what a wonderful image! – 'sheer silence'. God's presence speaks in reassurance that Elijah is not alone. The Psalmist says, 'Be still and know that I am God' (Psalm 46.10). This is the grace of the present moment.

Central to Jewish faith is the *Shema*, 'Hear O Israel, the Lord our God, the Lord is one; you shall love the Lord your God with all your heart, and with all your soul, and with all your mind, and with all your strength' (Deuteronomy 6.4f). These verses are to be said daily on rising and sleeping and taught diligently to children of the household. The words we associate with these are, 'you shall love your neighbour as yourself', which occur in another book of Moses (Leviticus 19.18). However, the two verses are not found together in the Hebrew Scriptures of Judaism, nevertheless in the Leviticus passage there is a command to love the self. This might be called respect and a self-care.

Christianity

The commandment which is found in the *Shema* is quoted by Jesus as the first commandment in answer to the question of a scribe, to which Jesus' reply is that the first commandment is, 'Hear O Israel, the Lord our God, the Lord is one; you shall love the Lord your God with all your heart, and with all your soul, and with all your mind, and with all your strength' (Mark 12.28–9); and Jesus goes on, 'The second commandment is this, "You shall love your neighbour as yourself"' (Mark 12.31), thus adding to the *Shema*. Jesus links directly and sequentially love of God, with neighbour and self, and adds, 'No other commandment is greater than these.' Taylor comments: '(It) brings together two widely separated commands…while each is warmly commended by the Rabbis, so far as is known, no one save Jesus has brought them together as the two regulative principles which sum up man's duty' (Taylor 1963, p.488). This is significant for the argument here in that Jesus seems to be asserting what we would call 'self-love'.

In 1965, a Christian scholar who was widely read at the time, Harry Williams, wrote of how he could only speak of things proved true in his own experience: 'Must we not therefore look for God in what we are, in the whole kaleidoscope of our personal experience? And in this sense would it be wrong to speak of a theology of the self?' (Williams 1965, pp.8–10). This was important in the 1960s. However, it is not the final word. Jesus spoke of following him as denying ourselves: 'For those who want to save their life will lose it, and those who lose their life for my sake and for the sake of the gospel will save it' (Mark 8.34–7). This seems to indicate that the self, created in the image of God (Genesis 1.26), is the work of God, and we find our true selves in God. God is at the centre. Ched Myers in his commentary on Mark writes:

> the argument of this second call to discipleship... Jesus has revealed that his messiahship means political confrontation with, not rehabilitation of, the imperial state. Those who wish to 'come after him' will have to identify themselves with his subversive program. The stated risk is that the disciples will face the test of loyalty under interrogation by state authorities. If 'self' is denied, the cross will be taken up, a metaphor for capital punishment on grounds of insurgency. Through these definitive choices...the disciple will 'follow Jesus'. (Myers 1988, 2015, p.247)

Jesus shows his need for 'taking time out' for 'stillness', at the age of 12 by staying in the temple, listening 'and asking them questions' (Luke 2.41–52). When found and questioned by his anxious parents, his response was 'Did you not know that I must be in my Father's house?' Through his listening in the temple, Luke says: 'Jesus increased in wisdom and in years, and in divine and human favour' (Luke 2.52). At the beginning of his public ministry, following his baptism, Jesus is driven out into the wilderness, 'and the angels waited on him' (Mark 1.13). This must have been a period of intense loneliness. Wilderness is a metaphor in the Scriptures, of the desert experience, of waiting on God and as the place where God might be found, yet wrestling with the demons of self-will. In the wilderness, Jesus wrestles with the calling he believed he received at his baptism.

Throughout Jesus' ministry, we discover 'in the morning, while it was still very dark, he got up and went out to a deserted place, and there he prayed'. Sometimes the writer states 'a lonely place' (Mark 1.35; 6.30; 7.24; Luke 5.16; Matthew 14.23). He taught, 'Come unto me, all of you who are tired and bear heavy loads, and I will give you rest' (Matthew 11.28). Jesus knew his need for silence. He is our model; if he knew this need how much more, as professionals working with bereaved children and adolescents, do we? On one occasion, after the news of John the Baptist's cruel death, Jesus says to his friends: 'Come away to a deserted place all by yourselves and rest a while' (Mark

6.31). The disciples too needed silence. Mark adds to this account: 'for many were coming and going, and they had no leisure even to eat'. There are insights in Vanstone's book, *The Stature of Waiting* (1982), of the dignity of Jesus' waiting while being handing over to those who arrested and tried him. There is patience, passivity, vulnerability and powerlessness, which was to become, in the crucifixion, part of God's redemptive creative presence in the world. In bereavement care there are some glimpses of this waiting. Vanstone comments: 'waiting can be the most intense and poignant of all human experiences – the experience which, above all others, strips us of affectation and self-deception and reveals to us the reality of our needs, our values, and ourselves' (Vanstone 1982, p.83). There is a wonderful children's book called *Jesus' Day Off*, which shows the playful relaxing Jesus (Nicholas 1998).

Islam

The Qur'an is for the Muslim the eternal Word of God. From childhood, the first prayer is said as a gift for God. It is recited at the start of the five prayer periods during the day. It states the submission to the will of God (the literal meaning of the word 'Islam'):

> The Opening,
> In the name of God the Merciful, the Compassionate,
> Praise belongs to God the Lord of all Being,
> the All-merciful, the All–compassionate, the Master of the Day of Doom.
> Thee only we serve, to Thee alone we pray for succour.
> Guide us in the straight path,
> the path of those whom Thou hast blessed,
> not of those against whom Thou art wrathful,
> nor of those who are astray.
>
> (Arberry 1964, p.1)

Prayer is the first of five pillars or principles of Islam; the regularity of saying the prayer five times a day remembering the presence of God means that God comes to dominate everything the individual thinks, does and feels. Islam lays the importance of the self and the self's relationship with God.

In Islam are the Sufi mystics one of which is the work of Rumi (1207–1273). His poetry and writings have inspired many.

The Guest House

This being human is a guest house
Every morning a new arrival.
A joy, a depression, a meanness,
some momentary awareness comes
as an unexpected visitor.
Welcome and entertain them all!
Even if they're a crowd of sorrows, who violently sweep your house
empty of its furniture,
still, treat each guest honourably.
He may be clearing you out
for some new delight.
The dark thought, the shame, the malice.
Meet them at the door laughing,
and invite them in
Be grateful for whoever comes,
because each has been sent
as guide from beyond.

(Rumi 2004)

Kahlil Gibran (1883–1931), though not a Muslim, was influenced by Christianity and Islam's Sufi tradition. Gibran understood the faiths of Judaism, Christianity and Islam as coming from a common root and so brothers of one another through the same Spirit. Kahlil's work has a great deal to say on inner stillness and the grace of the present moment. He thought of the soul walking all paths and unfolding itself 'like a lotus of countless petals' (Najjar 2008, pp.74–75).

Drawing together experience and cultural context leading to practical implications

Henri Nouwen (1932–1996) was a Roman Catholic priest and theologian eventually working with Jean Vanier in Daybreak, the L'Arche community in Ontario, Canada. Nouwen had some wise words to say about being ourselves:

Often we want to be somewhere other than where we are, or even to be someone other than who we are. We tend to compare ourselves constantly with others and wonder why we are not as rich, as intelligent, as simple, as generous or as saintly as they are. Such comparisons make us feel guilty, ashamed or jealous. It is very important to realize that our vocation is hidden in where we are, and who we are. We are unique human beings, each with a call to realize in our own life what nobody else can, and to realize it in the concrete context of the here and now. We will never find our vocations by trying to figure out whether we are better or worse than others. We are good enough to do what we are called to do…be yourself! (Nouwen 1994)

Burn-out comes when, 'we are always doing something, talking, reading, listening to the radio, planning what next. The mind is kept naggingly busy on some easy, unimportant external things all day' (Ueland in Cameron 1995, p.87). This burn-out occurs across the professions. Stress can be a particular challenge to those working in the area of death, dying and bereavement. It is important to be a resource to yourself, accept yourself as you are and to love yourself. As with any mature person it is foolish to be a workaholic; that way leads to burn-out. Self-care needs to be physical, mental and spiritual.

Physical

Exercise is important. It may be walking with others, with the dog, on one's own and taking in the infinite variety of nature. It could be visiting the gym, Pilates, yoga, Zumba, keep fit or swimming. It might be seasonal games such as playing football, cricket, tennis or badminton. With games, there is the added benefit that these are social occasions.

Mental

This can mean relaxing, reading, visiting the theatre or participation in music, which can totally absorb a person: singing in a choir or playing an instrument alone or in a group. Attending a performance by a choir or orchestra, listening to a concert on a CD, DVD or the radio, and being so totally absorbed means that the carer can be taken outside themselves, into another world, an experience of the transcendent or numinous. For some this comes from reading or writing poetry.

The poet Rainer Maria Rilke (1875–1926) has much to say to support the carer. Rilke suggests that the carer needs to be patient with him/herself since there may be unresolved questions, however one day the answer may become clear. For example, today a stillborn child causes great distress to the parents leaving many unanswered questions.

Later the parents find there is research on stillbirths and recognise how many parents are affected, or parents with such questions find the organisation which supports bereaved parents called SANDS (Still and Neonatal Death Support) and find some answers to their tragedy. The contemporary poet Mary Oliver has much to offer, for example her thought-provoking poem 'Wild Geese', which is full of natural metaphors (see Astley 2006, p.28).

We are all creative people, created in the image and likeness of God our Creator. There are a myriad ways to create: improvising a piece of music, composing, writing poetry/a story, creating a meal, drawing/painting a picture, making a piece of furniture, making a tapestry, sailing, designing and creating a garden, decorating a room, building a boat…try it! The carer can lose herself in creativity. It is a way of being restored. A useful book is *The Artist's Way: A Course in Discovering and Recovering Your Creative Self* (Cameron 1995).

Play is about becoming so totally engrossed in an activity that time stands still. Children are experts at play. The American post-Christian theologian, Mary Daly (1928–2010) said play 'is the creative potential itself in human beings that is the image of God'. Remember the 'mars bar' philosophy; the advertisement at one time said 'a mars bar a day helps you work, rest and play'.

Spiritual

Parker Palmer, an educator and founder of the Center for Courage and Renewal, in his older days ponders the resurrection that takes place under the most destructive circumstances and comments on the 'vast web of life in which body and spirit are one' and asks 'if flesh and earth were not infused with spirit, how could we and the natural world be so full of beauty, healing and grace?' (Palmer 2015).

Meditation is a way of praying. Christians might use the Jesus Prayer: 'Lord Jesus Christ, son of the living God, be merciful to me a sinner' and continually repeat it, so that the person becomes part of the prayer. A breathing meditation is a slow intake of breath counting up to five and then letting the breath release counting to five and repeating this. An object such as a seashell, an ear of wheat, a seed can be felt and experienced by each of the senses in silent contemplation. It is helpful to have an object such as this in each room of your home. Walking itself can be an exercise in meditation; if you walk home use one of your senses to be aware of the environment around you – centering on a sense, for example sight on one day and hearing the next. This is one of the techniques in mindfulness which is worth looking at as a resource in a stressful job (there are many exercises on Google which can also be found on YouTube).

Find ways to switch off from the day on the way home from the workplace. One way is to focus on a good thing that happened during the day and simply reflect on it, letting the positive vibes sink in. Some carers like to switch on a CD or the car radio on the way home – and even sing along to it. Another idea is to change into 'play clothes', that is something different from work clothes, when you get home.

George Herbert (1593–1633), a thinker and a hymn writer, wrote the words below. They can be applied to any household activity, such as washing up, which can become a 'de-stresser' when done mindfully, as we watch the rainbow bubbles from the washing-up liquid.

> Teach me my God and King
> in all things thee to see;
> and what I do in anything
> to do it as for thee
> a servant with this cause
> makes drudgery divine;
> who sweeps a room, as for thy laws,
> makes that and the action fine.

Brother Lawrence (1614–1681) was a Carmelite lay brother in a monastery near Paris. He worked in the kitchen cleaning pots and making them shine and mending the sandals of the brothers. His thoughts were written in a book called *The Practice of the Presence of God.* One saying was, 'we ought not to be weary of doing things for the love of God who regards not the greatness of the work, but the love with which it is performed'.

ACTIVITIES TO ELICIT THE READER'S EXPERIENCE

A Life Line

Think back on your life; you may want to choose two decades which for various reasons were challenging for you, or do a chart of your whole life. With this information draw a time line of your life showing clearly what were the highs and the lows for you. It could look something like a temperature chart. When you have finished, compare the highs and the lows. Which predominate and why? Later you are invited to share it with someone who is responsible for you as a carer: your mentor or supervisor.

What resources do you have?

Imagine yourself as a tree. A tree has roots which stretch down and give nurture to the tree and a trunk which is solid with branches stretching out to the future. Draw or cut out and stick a picture of a tree on a large sheet of paper. On the roots write all that nurtures and provides resources for you as a person and a professional. The trunk is your present moment; on here you could write your current out-of-work commitments to family members and friends. The branches stretching out are symbolic of the work that you do; it may include listening, mentoring, teaching, advising and administrative work.

Look at the finished work and comment on what you have discovered. Show it to a mentor and invite that person's comments.

9

Weaving the Threads Together

A man was travelling alone through the Himalayas. The scenery was spectacular but isolated. Suddenly he came across a bare hut surrounded by growing vegetables tendered by an old man. Each acknowledged the other and conversation began. The traveller asked, 'How do you live in such poverty, with so little?' The old man responded, 'But you have so little – just your back-pack.' The traveller replied, 'Oh yes, but I'm only on a journey.' 'So am I,' replied the old man.

(Traditional)

Experience

I quote verbatim to illustrate, with permission, a conversation between a friend and her grandson, Timothy, who is just five.

Granny: Do you know what is special about this Saturday?

Silence.

Granny: It's my birthday!

Timothy: Oh yes, and you'll be 61.

Granny: Can you remember my party last year when I was 60?

Timothy: Yes…and next year you'll be 62, then 63 then…(and he went on…right up to 100), but most people don't get to 100 do they?

Granny: Well, some people don't.

Timothy: Do you want to die, Granny?

Granny: Well, we all have to die some time, and some people when they get old, if they can't talk or walk or go the toilet on their own, they think it is easier to be dead than to be alive.

Timothy: But will you be able to breathe when you're dead?

Granny: No, but you won't need to be able to. It's only the body that needs to breathe, and it's only the body that dies. I think the bit of us that is deep down in us that makes us all special and different may live somewhere special when the body has stopped breathing, somewhere peaceful, maybe like being asleep or being in the best place you can think of that you've ever been to.

Timothy: Oh… So, are we having pasta for tea?

Reflection on experience

The lively conversation between five-year-old Timothy and his granny about her birthday, her increasing age and her eventual death arose because Timothy had tried to talk to his mum about death, which he had become aware of and wanted to understand, but his mother silenced him. It was not a suitable subject for a child. At the time,

Granny did not know this. She later explained to her daughter in law what had happened.

Linking adult, child and adolescent experience: concluding thoughts

Children are fascinated by death; they see a dead bird as did Stephanie in Chapter 1 and think that they can 'resurrect' it. Children want to know more. They ask questions so that they can relate a new experience to their existing knowledge. Sometimes they make mistakes and draw incorrect conclusions but then they try again and ask another question. Alice Jolly's son had a considerable number of questions to ask when his new sister was stillborn: 'How could she grow in the ground?' 'Can we buy another baby?' These questions were much to the consternation of his grieving mother, yet were real issues to him (see Chapter 3).

Those addressed in this book include a broad group of people with many life skills in human caring: parents; teachers; children and youth workers; those in voluntary work with children and adolescents; the medical profession and nursing; funeral directors; social workers; and ordained ministry and clergy. The book is also intended for those training for these professions. As professionals we need to learn to work alongside one another, to support and help each other. All are involved in the care of grieving and bereaved children and young people, yet we also need to be cared for, since this is a sensitive long-term relationship with the other.

Children have been called 'our spiritual giants'. Their insights are amazing. As adults, we can learn from children's attitudes of being open, up front, direct, unfazed by tradition or 'taboos'. They accept that death is natural and we need to learn to accept our mortality and live. Yes, we can and should be there beside children and adolescents who face the death of someone they are close to and love. They grieve and young children need to be reassured and comforted, adolescents listened to and sometimes consoled.

We need to recognise that children do grieve, but 'puddle jump' in and out of grief. Adolescents grieve but often in silence, needing their own space but also to know that there can be a listening ear. We are involved in helping them to learn that life is for living. We should also help them to ask the big questions in life and learn how to live to find the answers; for some these will be found by faith in human nature and for others through a faith in the love that we can call God.

The aim of this book is to be a theoretical and practical resource. The objective of the book is to encourage reflective practice arising from working with children and adolescents in their experiences associated with dying, bereavement and the afterlife. I have encouraged you, the reader, to interact with the contents: 'to enter into a conversation' with me, the writer. I have aimed to encourage you to learn more about this area of experience, to relate it to your own professional experience, to critically reflect on that experience and become more informed and confident in your practice of care. Please also use the website dyingtolive.org.uk to share conversations and comments.

Appendix 1

Creating a School Policy for the Pastoral Care of Bereaved Pupils

Having a policy in a school helps when a bereavement arises, particularly with sudden, multiple or traumatic circumstances. (The Critical Incident Procedure is the prerogative of the head teacher.)

The policy needs to be a framework rather than prescriptive and agreed by school staff (teaching and non teaching) and the governors (parent governors are particularly helpful as 'sounding boards').

The area of 'loss' is particularly emotive and sensitive and therefore needs a policy statement which is sensitive to each unique situation of loss. It is likely that a policy may need to be formulated in the same format as other policies in your school so the information below is a suggestion only.

It is important that the policy is regularly reviewed in the light of experience.

The idea of such a policy is included within the Department for Education and Skills (2005) *Common Core of Skills and Knowledge for the Children's Workforce*. This document sets out the areas of expertise which anyone whose work brings them into frequent contact with children should have. The six areas include 'Supporting transitions', which states that 'some children may have to face very particular and personal transitions not necessarily shared or understood by all their peers. These include: family illness or the death of a close relative' (p.16).

A school policy is likely to include the following:

- aim

- rationale

- clear guidance on procedures

- emphasis on confidentiality

- reference to outside support systems and resources

- review structures.

The ideas below are to encourage discussion and the construction of a policy reflecting the needs of your particular school.

Aim

A policy on the pastoral care of pupil(s) and the school community in the event of loss through bereavement.

Rationale

To work as appropriate with pupil(s) with their consent and that of the family to give ongoing care of pupils following a bereavement.

Guidance on procedures – some considerations

Personnel, defining roles and responsibilities. In a primary school, everyone will be involved.

- Identify one person to take overall responsibility. This may well be the head teacher (plus a deputy to cover absence), who receives news of a death and informs staff; in some schools this is done using email.

- The accuracy of the information concerning a death should always be checked (sometimes rumour can abound; it is necessary to check the facts).

- It is important to consult and follow up with the family and, if appropriate, the pupil.

- There needs to be a clear set of ground rules of do's and don't's for all teachers concerning bereavement. Respect for the child and confidentiality are paramount.

- A policy for consulting the bereaved pupil (and the family) and one relating to how the information is handled, e.g. for telling (or not telling) a peer group when a pupil is absent due to the death of a parent.

- A policy of strategies for coping with pupils who become distressed in class – e.g. a yellow card (to signal that the pupil needs to leave the room).

- A policy to ensure communication with parents.

A policy/guidelines should address 'types' of death which involve different responses:

- the death of a parent of a pupil

- a pupil/teacher with a terminal illness on long-term sick leave and the information given

- a traumatic incident

- the death of a member of staff

- is the policy known, so that pupils/staff know who to talk to if they need a listening ear?

A policy covers record keeping:

- the necessity of checking sensitively the facts

- keeping records

- place and accessibility of records (for new members of staff; a child changing class).

A policy needs to recognise the long-term effects of bereavement in regard to:

- behaviour of pupils

- support services if bereavement issues persist and appear to becoming 'pathological'; knowing who to refer to

- a calendar (or similar) which is marked to show significant anniversaries of the death, where sensitivity will be needed by the school.

Materials to support staff and pupils: books/ videos

Decisions will need to be made on:

- where books (on loss and death) for pupils are kept

- who services materials, keeping them available and up to date

- training and support of staff working with bereavement needs to be addressed.

Reference to outside support systems

A designated person is useful to take responsibility for the following:

- lists and copies of support agencies

- decisions on where these are kept.

Review structures

- The policy needs to be reviewed regularly

- All staff need to be inducted in the policy.

Appendix 2

Creating a School Policy: Exploring Loss through the Curriculum

Ofsted inspectors look for Spiritual, Moral, Social and Cultural development throughout the curriculum.

The educational aspect of this area is likely to include:

- knowledge, e.g. recognition of different losses, rites of passage, beginnings and endings, cultural differences, funeral practices, irreversibility of death

- skills, e.g. handling emotions, dealing with anger

- attitudes, e.g. positive – death is natural; life is for living and enjoying.

Questions for the subject of 'loss' in the curriculum

- Is there a clear rationale and aims for the exploration of loss through the curriculum?

- How do these aims support the overall aims of the schools?

- Are there clear principles for the exploration of loss through the curriculum?

- How do these principles support the 4 Every Learner principles:

  - access and entitlement

  - curricular balance

  - differentiation and potential

  - preparation for the future?

Planning for the curriculum

- Is a particular teacher identified to coordinate work on loss within the school?

- Does the policy explain how work on loss is planned in a systematic way?

- Does the policy make clear how different subjects and other curricular activities contribute to a growing awareness and understanding of loss?

- Does the policy make clear how work on loss is linked to bereavement support?

- Does the policy indicate the range of resources available to support work on death?

- Does the policy make clear how continuity and progression are catered for in relation to work on loss?

- Does the policy make clear how work on loss is to be monitored and evaluated?

Work on loss may feature in informal ways

- circle time – sharing news; pupils discussing something seen on the TV

- a pupil approaching a pastoral member of staff (who has been trained in listening/counselling skills)

- incidental conversations, for example in the dinner queue or before lessons with teaching and non-teaching members of staff and other pupils

- following something said in assembly

- following a publicised traumatic incident (e.g. a tsunami)

- story time.

Loss may be addressed formally through the curriculum

This will be academic and intellectually rigorous but will also include the emotions and the social effects of loss. Death should be seen as natural and part of life through:

- the changing seasons of the year – the growth of plants, trees losing leaves in Autumn; pupils planting bulbs

- life cycles in animals – insects such as the butterfly; spawn/ tadpole/ frog; humans from pregnancy – looking at scan photos and seeing a newborn baby and its growth

- mourning little losses – e.g. a lost tooth; a lost or broken toy; a cancelled outing. It is important that the different grief reactions to these losses are respected

- keeping pets – mourning the death of a pet by having a 'funeral'; talking about it, listening and acknowledging the sadness

- expressing emotions connected with loss – e.g. losing a friend when you move house or school, divorce (great care is needed here – but children will express a range of emotions in school to such happenings)

- reading stories which use concepts of loss and death (see Further Reading lists)

- acknowledging deaths of significant people on the TV and in the media

- teachers and parents being able to show and share their own feelings with children; being honest; acting as a model for children when they encounter losses in their own lives

- talking of memories of someone important to our lives

- visiting a local church and looking at the gravestones

- expressing feelings about the death of someone known to all the children, e.g. a teacher/auxiliary/pupil in a suitable way:

    - making a card for the family

- drawing a picture

- writing their memories down to send to the bereaved

- preparing a special assembly

- planting a tree (always plant two in case one dies).

Personal, Health, Social and Moral Education (PHSME)

- life skills, dealing with emotional effects of loss

- learning skills, memory scrapbook

- relationships including separations

- consideration of and debate on organ donation

- visit to/have a speaker from/support a hospice

- exploration of extending life through a healthy lifestyle.

Appendix 3

The Nature of Childhood

The sociologist Philippe Ariès and the historian Hugh Cunningham have detailed the developing understanding of childhood noting historical changes in ideas about concepts of stages of development, the portrayal of children in pictures, children's dress, the history of games and the notion that children were naturally innocent and in need of protection. Ariès came to the conclusion that the development of universal education had 'created' childhood (Ariès 1979). Change had come about in many ways. The ancient Greeks saw children as irrational since they were without speech; children surviving childhood were incorporated into adult life: everyone had a part to play and children were not distinctive or treated any differently; they were simply immature adults, important not for their present but their future value. The Enlightenment's emphasis on rationality created a category of irrational persons, 'children', who needed training and correction; gradually education was seen as significant for all. A pivotal moment was the Education Act of 1870.

Cunningham (2006) noted the changes in work patterns from agriculture based around the home in the sixteenth and seventeenth centuries to the industrialisation in the cities of the eighteenth and nineteenth centuries with children working in domestic service, in mines and factories and climbing chimneys. This was seen as encouraging the habit of work and moral principles. Gradually, child labour was realised to be exploitative and subsequently regulated. Later the idea of a 'natural childhood' took root. Children came to be seen as in need of protection and guidance within a family. Thus in Victorian times, and before, the presence of children at a death was seen as normal. Changes have continued in what is called the 'social construct' of childhood. The education of children is now a lengthy commitment with socialisation taking place in the home.

Appendix 4

Babies and Infants Dying

A brief history, some case studies and ensuing ethical issues.

History

Throughout history, it is likely that infanticide, the deliberate killing of newborns with consent of parents and the community, was known, yet euthanasia meaning 'a good death' was a practice of allowing the patient to die in peace and with dignity. For the physician, it meant caring for the patient and preventing pain and suffering, though in ancient times physicians could either heal or cause the death of a patient by providing a poison. Hippocrates (460–375 BCE) challenged the practice of poisons since they destroyed life, an end alien to medicine, his professionalism included establishing a set of ethical principles defining the physician as healer, the Hippocratic oath, with the principle of primum non nocere (first, do no harm). Hippocrates is traditionally regarded as the father of Western medicine (Edelstein 1967).

The Greek city-states and ancient Rome saw infanticide as a way of ridding themselves of deformed babies by exposing them. Plato (424–347 BCE) was an advocate of infanticide for eugenic purposes. It served as a form of birth control when food was scarce for the Eskimos, the Kung in Africa and in eighteenth century Japan.

However, the monotheistic religions of Judaism, Christianity and Islam condemned infanticide as murder. The commandments taught that human life is sacred, a gift from God and not to be destroyed, a teaching reflected in the sixth commandment (Exodus 21.13); today, particularly in the United States, this belief is central to moral consciousness. All human life is of equal value, and all humans have a right to life.

However, in the twentieth century, in the Netherlands and Belgium in the heart of Christian Europe, following lengthy debate about the suffering of babies and infants, euthanasia was legalised. It could include a baby born with anencephaly, a condition with most of the brain missing, which occurs in about one in every 2,000 births; while biologically human the baby will never 'develop rudimentary consciousness, let alone an ability to relate to others or a sense of the future' (Holt 2005). The legislation also covered infants and children suffering uncontrollable pain with a terminal illness.

The viability of babies

Babies born pre-term, whose organs were not totally formed, would die before or at birth. Gestational age is the primary determinant of almost all perinatal outcomes; '22 weeks is considered to be the cut-off for human viability and for week 25 onwards there is a general agreement that active management should be offered' (Royal College of Obstetricians and Gynaecologists 2014). Today the charity Bliss (www.bliss.org.uk) is a source of information and an advocate for babies born pre-term. It states that one in nine babies born in the UK will spend at least a few days in a neonatal unit which specialises in the care of preterm, small and sick babies. Parents, particularly mothers, are supported on a neonatal unit, since sadly some babies are too small and do not survive.

Babies born with disabilities and abnormalities

Across much of Europe in the 1960s, children were born with deformities, their condition traced to the thalidomide drug taken in pregnancy. A BBC TV programme, 'The Midwives', based on diaries of the period, showed the anguish of the GPs who unwittingly prescribed the drug and the doctors delivering the babies. On such occasions the baby was fed, kept warm and allowed to die. Parents were not consulted in the decision. Today, in countries of the developing world, children with disabilities are more likely to be abandoned and left to die for lack of adequate facilities.

In developed countries, doctors are convinced that, 'there is a clear difference between active and passive euthanasia – killing and letting die – yet a defendable ethical difference is hard to find' (Gillert 1998).

Infants are still left for nature to take its course.

Ethical issues

Care of very sick children

There are children's hospices in many countries today and these are places of joy and laughter, caring for babies to young people up to the age of 18. They support families, children and young people living with life-threatening conditions from diagnosis to end of life and throughout bereavement. This is done through a range of services delivered where the family wishes – in the home, at hospital, in the community or at the hospice. The help is not simply when death is imminent, care at the end of life is not the only service provided. Many children and young people using the service are extremely active but need additional support and care as their conditions develops. Within some hospices there are play specialists helping a child to grow in confidence and aid their physical and mental wellbeing, sensory rooms providing art and music sessions, places to interact and share. Support extends to include families, parents and siblings since the hospice staff recognise the stress of living with a life-threatening illness.

Euthanasia

In the Netherlands and Belgium, where euthanasia is permitted by law, there is debate about methods, which are varied and controversial. One method is that of an intravenous sedative to silence the brain, followed by a morphine injection which is a pain medication. This can trigger respiratory arrest and death; if it does not neuromuscular blockers are added causing death in 5-10 minutes. Eduard Verhagen, head of the Department of Paediatrics at Groningen, in the Netherlands, states, 'It happens in a peaceful manner' (quoted in Nuwer 2014).

An alternative to this proactive method of euthanasia is that of palliative care such as the withdrawal of food and fluid. In the UK, this was known in the 1990s as the Liverpool Care Pathway (LCP); it was used under the supervision of the medical team, in the case of terminally ill adults. However, families claimed that their relatives were denied food and drink, leaving them to 'linger in misery for weeks'. The Care Minister, Norman Lamb, announced an independent review, chaired by Baroness Julia Neuberger and published in July 2013. Accepting the review's recommendations, the government advised that NHS hospitals should phase out the use of the LCP over the next 6–12 months. This method has been used with babies and infants with varying results. A doctor commented that parents and care teams do not realise the average time from withdrawal of hydration to death, which can be ten days or more. Nor were parents prepared for the changes in the infant's physical appearance – due to dehydration – 'the unique horror of witnessing a child become smaller and shrunken' (quoted in Ertelt 2012).

In the UK a judge allowed a mother, Charlotte Wise, to refuse food or water to her 12-year-old daughter, Nancy, who had been born blind with hydorcephalus. At birth, she required 24-hour care, and was fed, watered and medicated by tube at Great Ormond Street Hospital in London. Since her mother had taken her home Nancy's health had begun to deteriorate, and she would scream in agony despite morphine and ketamine. Her mother 'knew' her suffering was too much and that Nancy deserved to be at peace and had a right to die. When drink was withdrawn, Nancy's death took fourteen days, distressing Charlotte. It is interesting that it was the mother's decision to go to court and seek permission based on her assumption that Nancy wanted to die; however it needs to be recognised that it is possible that Nancy could neither understand nor show her thoughts. Does the legal verdict raise a precedent and indicate a need for a change in law to allow euthanasia?

The arguments for and against euthanasia are given in detail on a BBC website www.bbc.co.uk/ethics/euthanasia/against/against_1.shtml.

The situation in the USA
The Ohio Pediatrics Ethics Survey of 1993 asked 900 parents about keeping children alive, who medical science would not previoulsy have been able to; this was in the light of limited funds for health care. Parents were asked to respond to scenarios such as: If your child was seriously injured in an accident and the medical team states that your child is likely to be severely brain damaged and dependent on you for the remainder of his/her life would you want:

1. 'everything' done

2. a do not ressussitate (DNR) order

3. withdrawal of potentially life sustaining machines

4. withdrawal of all support including nutrition

5. a lethal injection of a sedative to be given ('mercy killing').

The survey ended with the questions:

Do you support physician-supported suicide (voluntary death)? Yes or No

Do you support 'mercy killing' (non-voluntary death)? Yes or No

Although the survey received no attention outside the Cleveland area it sent a message to those 900 parents: euthanasia for a child is an option that deserves attention[1].

Laws about euthanasia for adults have never reached the statue books, yet were written in Wisconsin (1975), Iowa (1989) and Illinois (1997). By 2014, Oregon, Vermont, Washington and Montana allowed physician assisted suicide under strict and detailed legislation; California is likely to pass legislation in 2016. Thirty eight states prohibit assisted suicide. It is not considered for children, although on occasions the law is challenged by particular cases, for example that of Natalie in Texas. Natalie, at 19 months, fell into the family swimming pool. She was rushed into a children's hospital but when she awoke Natalie had lost sight, hearing and movement; her organs began to fail. Brad, her grandfather said he began to 'think that dreadful thought: we can't let her live like this'. Doctors decided to allow the feeding tube to be removed and sent her home. Brad asked if that wasn't starving her to death and wondered why the doctors couldn't give her an injection such as morphine – peaceful and quick. Deprived of food and water, Natalie died after nine days. Brad described the death as 'pure torture...just the most cruel, inhumane thing'. The family is now campaigning for the state to legalise euthanasia (Johnson 2014).

The American College of Pediatricians have produced a useful and insightful paper 'Neonatal Euthanasia: the Groningen Protocol' in response to the Netherlands. The abstract states:

An examination of the criteria used by the Protocol to justify the euthanasia of seriously ill neonates reveals the criteria are not based on firm moral principles. The taking of life of a seriously ill person is not the solution to pain and suffering of the dying process. It is the role of the medical profession to care for the ailing patient with love

---

1   www.patientsrightscouncil.org/site/not-for-adults-only

and compassion, always preserving the person's dignity. Neonatal euthanasia is not ethically permissible. (Vizcarrondo 2014)

Summary

The acceptance of infanticide for neonates, infants and young people and the methods used vary widely across Europe and the United States. Rachel Nuwer, writing in the *New Scientist* (2014), concludes:

> for most parts of the world, a refusal to even discuss the subject dominates. As unpleasant as it is, parents, physicians, hospitals and nations need to confront this issue as a matter of responsibility towards both infants born into hopeless circumstances and their families.

References

Abdel Haleem, M.A.S. (2004) *The Qur'an: A New Translation*. Oxford: Oxford University Press.

Aha Parenting (n.d.) 'Explaining death to children'. Available at www.ahaparenting.com/ask-the-doctor-1/explaining-death-to-children, accessed on 21 March 2016.

Albom, M. (2003) *The Five People You Meet in Heaven*. London: Little Brown Publishers.

Ariès, P. (1974) *Western Attitudes toward Death: From the Middle Ages to the Present*. Baltimore, MD and London: Johns Hopkins University Press.

Barr, J. (1992) *The Garden of Eden and the Hope of Immortality*. London: SCM Press.

Billings, A. (2002) *Dying and Grieving: A Guide to Pastoral Ministry*. London: SPCK.

Bowker, J. (1983) *Worlds of Faith*. Ariel Books. London: BBC Books.

Brown D.A. (1975) *A Guide to Religions*. London: SPCK.

Burgess, R. (2003) *Children at Funerals*. Glasgow: Wild Goose Publications.

Cameron, J. (1995) *The Artist's Way: A Course in Discovering and Recovering Your Creative Self*. London, Basingstoke and Oxford: Pan Macmillan.

Carle, E. (2002) *The Very Hungry Caterpillar*. London: Puffin Penguin Publishers.

Child Bereavement UK (n.d) School's Information Pack. Available at http://shop.childbereavement.org/schools-information-pack-135-p.asp, accessed on 7 June 2016.

Child Bereavement Trust, The (2000) *The Child Bereavemnt Trust Workbook*.

Church of England (2000) *Common Worship: Pastoral Services*. London: Church House Publishing.

Church Times, The (2014) 'How teens can deal well with death.' Available at www.churchtimes.co.uk/articles/2014/22-august/comment/opinion/how-teens-can-deal-well-with-death, accessed 27 May 2016.

Cohen, J. (ed.) (2001) *Caring Classrooms/Intelligent Schools: The Social Emotional Education of Young Children*. Series on Social Emotional Learning. New York: Teachers College Press.

ComRes (2014) *'Dying Matters Public Attitudes to Bereavement Survey.'* Survey on behalf of Dying Matters Coalition, 10 December.

Commission on Religion and Belief in British Public Life (2015) *Living with Difference: Community, Diversity and the Common Good*. Cambridge: Woolf Institute.

Conze, E. (trans.) (1959) *The Buddhist Scripture*. Harmondsworth: Penguin.

Cranwell, B. (2007) 'Making death into an adults-only affair.' *Church Times*. 29 June.

Crossley, D. (2000) *Muddles, Puddles and Sunshine*. Gloucester: Winston's Wish Publications.

Davie, G. (2000) *Religion in Modern Europe: A Memory Mutates*. Oxford: Oxford University Press.

Davies, D. (2008) *The Theology of Death*. London and New York: T&T Clark.

de Hennezel, M. (1997) *The Intimate Death: How the Dying Teach Us to Live*. London: Little Brown.

de Lange, N. (1987) *Judaism*. Oxford and New York: Oxford University Press.

Diamond, J. (1998) *Because Cowards Get Cancer Too: A Hypochrondriac Confronts His Nemesis*. London: Times Books.

Dougy Center, The: The National Center for Grieving Children and Families (2008) *Helping the Grieving Student: A Guide for Teachers*. Portland, OR: The Dougy Center.

Draper, A. (2008) *Good Grief: What Will We Tell the Kids?* West Hertfordshire Primary Care Trust. Available at www.thegrid.org.uk/learning/hwb/ewb/resources/documents/good_grief.pdf, accessed on 14 March 2016.

Duffy, W. (2008) *Children and Bereavement*. London: Church House Publishing.

Edelstein, L. (1967) *The Hippocratic Oath: Text, Translation and Interpretation.* Baltimore, MD: John Hopkins University Press.

Ertelt, S. (2012) 'Doctor's haunting testimony: UK babies put on euthanasia pathway.' *International Lifenews*, November 9. Available at www.lifenews.com/2012/11/29/doctors-haunting-testimony-uk-babies-put-on-euthanasia-pathway, accessed on 04 May 2016.

Feifel, H. (1959) *The Meaning of Death.* New York: McGraw-Hill.

Francis, L.J. and Slee, N. (1996) *Autumn: Betsy Bear Learns about Death.* Birmingham: National Christian Education Council.

Gillert, G. (1998) 'Euthanasia, letting die and the pause.' *Journal of Medical Ethics 14,2,* 61-68.

Gould, P. (2012) *When I Die: Lessons from the Death Zone.* London: Little Brown.

Graham, J.A. (2013) 'How do children comprehend the concept of death?' *Psychology Today.* Available at www.psychologytoday.com/blog/hard-realities/201301/how-do-children-comp, accessed on 21 March 2016.

Griffiths, G. (2010) *Goodbye Baby: Cameron's Story.* Edinburgh: St Andrew Press.

Guild of St Raphael, Children's Hospice (2002) 'Whose side is God on?' *Chrism.* Available at www.guild-of-st-raphael.org.uk/topics-childrenhospice.htm, accessed on 21 March 2016.

Hauerwas, S. (1990) *Naming the Silences: Medicine and the Problem of Suffering.* New York and London: T&T Clark.

Hick, J. 'Reincarnation.' In A. Richardson and J. Bowden (eds) (1989) *A New Dictionary of Christian Theology*, 5th edn. London: SCM Press.

Hilpern, K. (2013) 'Should young children go to funerals?' The Guardian, 12 July 2013. Available at http://www.theguardian.com/lifeandstyle/2013/jul/12/should-young-children-go-to-funerals, accessed on 8 June 2016.

Hitchens, C. (2012) *Mortality.* London: Atlantic Books.

Holt, J. (2005) 'Euthanasia for babies?' *The New York Times Magazine*, 07 October. Available at www.nytimes.com/2005/07/10/magazine/euthanasia-for-babies.html, accessed on 05 May 2016.

Intergovernmental Panel on Climate Change (2013) *Climate Change 2013: The Physical Science Basis.* Available at www.ipcc.ch/report/ar5/wg1/, accessed on 27 May 2016.

Hospice Foundation of America (1990) *Interview with Dr. J. William Worden.* Hospice Foundation of America. Available at http://hospicefoundation.org/Professionals/Experts-Talk-EOL-Care/Interview-with-Dr-J-William-Worden, accessed 27 May 2016.

Jalland, P. (2013) 'Changing Cultures of Grief 1850–1970.' In S. Oliver (ed.) *Inside Grief.* London: SPCK.

James, H. (2004) *A Fitting End: Making the Most of a Funeral.* Norwich: Canterbury Press.

Janney, J. (2002) *Milly's Bug-nut.* Gloucester: Winston's Wish Publications.

Job, N. and Francis, G. (2004) *Childhood Bereavement: Developing the Key and Pastoral Support.* London: National Children's Bureau.

Johnson, B. (2014) 'Family that starved baby to death pushing Texas to legalize euthanasia.' *Lifesite News*, 28 March 2014. Available at https://www.lifesitenews.com/news/family-that-starved-baby-to-death-pushing-texas-to-legalize-euthanasia, accessed 27 May 2016.

Kelly, E. (2008) *Meaningful Funerals Meeting the Theological and Pastoral Challenge in a Postmodern Era.* London and New York: Mowbray.

Levine, S. (1986) *Who Dies? An Investigation of Conscious Living and Conscious Dying.* New York: Anchor Books.

Liddle, M. and Solanki, A-R. (2002) *Persistent Young Offenders: Research on Individual Backgrounds, and Life Experiences.* London: National Association for Care & Resettlement of Offenders, NACRO.

Luft, J. and Ingham, H. (1955) *The Johari Window: A Graphic Model of Interpersonal Awareness.* Los Angeles, CA: Proceedings of the Western Training Laboratory in Group Development.

Magonet, J. (2004) *A Rabbi Reads the Bible.* London: SCM Press.

Marshall, E. (2003) *Kids Talk about Heaven.* London: Kyle Cathie Ltd.

Mellonie, B. and Ingpen, R. (1983) *Lifetimes: The Beautiful Way to Explain Death to Children.* New York: Bantam Books.

Moltmann, J. (1996) *The Coming of God: Christian Eschatology.* London: SCM Press.

Myers, C. (1988, 2015) *Binding the Strong Man: A Political Reading of Mark's Story of Jesus.* Maryknoll, NY: Orbis Books.

Najjar, A. (2008) *Kahlil Gibran: A Biography.* London: Saqi Books.

Neuberger, J. (1999) *Dying Well: A Guide to Enabling a Good Death.* Hale: Hochland and Hochland.

New York Times (1939) '"Mercy death" law ready for Albany.' February 14.

NICE Clinical Guidelines (2015) *Depression in Children and Young People: Identification and Management in Primary Community and Secondary Care.* Available at www.nice.org.uk/guidance/cg28, accessed on 21 March 2016.

Nicholas, A. (1998) *Jesus' Day Off.* London: Hutchinson Children's Books.

Nouwen, H. (1994) *The Wounded Healer: Ministry in Contemporary Society.* London: Darton, Longman and Todd.

Nuwer, R. (2014) 'The world needs to talk about child euthanasia.' *New Scientist,* 24 February. Available at https://www.newscientist.com/article/mg22129580-200-the-world-needs-to-talk-about-child-euthanasia, accessed on 4 May 2016.

Nuffield Council on Bioethics (2005) 'Critical care decisions in fetal and neonatal medicine: ethical issues.' London: Nuffield Council on Bioethics.

Oldfield, E., Hartnett, L. and Bailey, E. (2013) *More than an Educated Guess: Assessing the Evidence on Faith Schools.* London: Theos.

Opposing Views (n.d.) 'How to Proceed with Bereavement in Islam.' Available at http://people.opposingviews.com/proceed-bereavement-islam-8865.html, accessed on 27 May 2016.

Palmer, P.J. (2015) 'A wilderness pilgrimage: where we go when we die.' Available at www.onbeing.org/blog/parker-palmer-a-wilderness-pilgrimage-where-we-go-when-we-die/7869, accessed on 18 March 2016.

Parkes, P.M., Laungani, P. and Young, B. (eds) (1997) *Death and Bereavement Across Cultures.* London and New York: Routledge.

Perham, M. (1997) *New Handbook of Pastoral Liturgy.* London: SPCK.

Porter, M. (2015) *Grief is the Thing with Feathers.* London: Faber and Faber.

Reoch, R. (1997) *Dying Well: A Holistic Guide for the Dying and Their Carers.* Stroud: Hamlyn.

Remen, R. (2000) *My Grandfather's Blessings: Tales of Strength, Refuge and Belonging.* London: Thorsons.

Rhodes, B. (2013) 'Tell Me, "Which Way Ought I to Go from Here?" Supporting Those who Grieve in a Diverse Society.' In S. Oliver (ed.) *Inside Grief.* London: SPCK.

Robinson H. and Straky M. (2014) *The Cooper Tree.* London: Strauss House Publisher.

Royal College of Obstetricians and Gynaecologists (2005) 'Response of the Ethics Committee of the Royal College of Obstetricians and Gynaecologists to Nuffield Council on Bioethics consultation document *The ethics of prolonging life in fetuses and the newborn.*' Available at http://nuffieldbioethics.org/wp-content/uploads/Royal-College-of-Obstetricians-Gynaecologists.pdf, accessed 8 June 2016.

Royal College of Obstetricians and Gynaecologists (2014) Scientific Impact Paper no.41. 'Perinatal Management of Pregnant Women at the Threshold of Infant Viability.' February 2014.

Rumi, J. (2004) *Essential Rumi,* trans. C. Barks, J. Moyne, A. Arberry and R. Nicholson. San Francisco, CA: Harper Collins.

Syeed, A and Ritchie, N. (2005) 'Children and the Five Pillars of Islam: Practicing Spirituality in Daily Life' In M. Yust, A.N. Johnson, S.E. Sasso and E.C. Roehlkepartain (eds) *Nurturing Child and Adolescent Spirituality: Perspectives from the World's Religious Traditions.* Maryland: Rowman & Littlefield.

Schilder, P. and Wechsler, D. (1934) 'The attitude of children towards death.' *Journal of Genetic Psychology 45,* 406–51.

Schwartz, M. (1998) *Letting Go: Reflections on Living While Dying.* London: Pan Macmillan.

Sendak, M. (2000) *Where the Wild Things Are.* London: Red Fox Books.

Sheppy, P. (2003) *Death, Liturgy and Ritual,* Vol. 1. Aldershot: Ashgate Publishers.

Silverstein, S. (1964) *The Giving Tree.* London: Harper and Row.

Smid, E. (2015) *Luna's Red Hat: An Illustrated Storybook to Help Children Cope with Loss and Suicide.* London: Jessica Kingsley Publishers.

Smith, S. (1995, 1999) *The Forgotten Mourners: Guidelines for Working with Bereaved Children.* London: Jessica Kingsley Publishers.

Speece, M.W. (1995) 'Children's concepts of death.' *Michigan Family Review 1,* 1, 57–69.

Speece, M.W. and Brent, S.B. (1996) 'The Development of Children's Understanding of Death.' In C.A. Corr and D.M. Corr (eds) *Handbook of Childhood Death and Bereavement.* New York: Springer Publisher.

Stokes, J.A. (2005) *A Child's Grief*, 2nd edn. Gloucester: Winston's Wish Publications.

Stokes, J.A. (2006) *Out of the Blue: Making Memories Last When Someone has Died.* Gloucester: Winston's Wish Publications.

Stokes, J.A. (2009) *The Secret C– Straight Talking About Cancer*, 2nd edn. Gloucester: Winston's Wish Publications.

Taylor, V. (1963) *The Gospel According to St Mark.* London: Macmillan.

Tayyibun Weekday Hifdh School (n.d) Available at www.tayyibunmadrasah.co.uk/tayyibun--hifdh-school/, accessed in 27 May 2016.

Templeton, T. and Lumley, T. (2002) '9/11 in numbers.' The Guardian, 18 August 2002. Available at http://www.theguardian.com/world/2002/aug/18/usa.terrorism, accessed on 27 May 2016.

Varley, S. (1985, 1992) *Badger's Parting Gifts.* London: Picture Lions.

Vanstone, W.H. (1982) *The Stature of Waiting.* London: Darton, Longman and Todd.

Verhagen, J.E. and Sauer P.J. (2005) 'The Groningen Protocol – euthanasia in severely ill newborns.' *New England Journal of Medicine 352*, 190, 959–62.

Viorst, J. (1971, 1988) *The Tenth Good Thing about Barney.* New York: Aladdin Paperbacks, an imprint of Simon & Schuster.

Vizcarrondo, F.E, (primary author) (2014) 'Neonatal euthanasia: The Groningen Protocol.' *American College of Pediatricians.* Available at http://www.acpeds.org/the-college-speaks/position-statements/life-issues/neonatal-euthanasia-2, accessed on 27 May 2016.

Walter, T. (1999) *On Bereavement: The Culture of Grief.* Buckingham: Open University Press.

Weymont, D. and Rae, T. (2005) *Supporting Young People Coping with Grief, Loss and Death.* London: Sage Publications Ltd.

Wilkinson, A. (1978) *The Church of England and the First World War.* London: SPCK.

Williams, H.A. (1965) *The True Wilderness.* London: Constable.

Ward, B. (1993) *Healing Grief: A Guide to Loss and Recovery.* London: Vermilion.

Winston's Wish (2002) *A Child's Grief.* Gloucester: Winston's Wish Publishers.

Wolfe, I., Macfarlane, A., Donkin, A., Marmot, M. and Viner, R. (2014) *Why Children Die: Death in Infants, Children and Young People in the UK.* Royal College of Paediatrics and Child Health, National Children's Bureau and British Association for Child and Adolescent Public Health. Available at www.ncb.org.uk/media/1130496/rcpch_ncb_may_2014_-_why_children_die__part_a.pdf, accessed on 05 May 2016.

Woodhouse, P. (2009) *Etty Hillesum: A Life Transformed.* London: Continuum.

Worden, J.W. (1996) *Children and Grief: When a Parent Dies.* New York and London: Guilford Press.

Further Reading

Books for children

Under fives

Allsworth, A. (2008) *Remember Me Always: A Handbook to Help Bereaved Families Care for Grieving Children.* Redruth: Penhaligon's Friends.

Butler, H. (2014) *Us Minus Mum.* London: Little Brown Young Readers.

Carle, E. (2002) *The Very Hungry Caterpillar.* London: Puffin Penguin.

Francis, L.J. and Slee, N. (1996) *Autumn: Betsy Bear Learns about Death.* Birmingham: National Christian Education Council.

Gray, N. and Cabban, V. (2001) *Little Bear's Grandad.* London: Little Tiger Press.

Mellonie, B. and Ingpen, R. (1983) *Lifetimes: The Beautiful Way to Explain Death to Children.* New York: Bantam Books.

Rivett, R. (2009) *Are you Sad, Little Bear? A Book About Learning to Say Goodbye.* Oxford: Lion.

Rock, L. (2004) *When Goodbye is Forever.* Oxford: Lion Publishing House.

Sendak, M. (2000) *Where the Wild Things Are.* London: Red Fox Books.

Smid, E. (2015) *Luna's Red Hat. An Illustrated Storybook to Help Children Cope with Loss and Suicide.* London: Jessica Kingsley Publishers.

Varley, S. (1985, 1992) *Badger's Parting Gifts.* London: Picture Lions.

Viorst, J. (1971, 1988) *The Tenth Good Thing about Barney.* New York: Aladdin Paperbacks, an imprint of Simon & Schuster.

Key Stage 1 (five to seven years)

Earl, C. (n.d.) *My Grandad Plants People: A Simple Guide for Grown-Ups when Children Ask about Death.* Available at www.bereavementadvice.org/topics/the-funeral/taking_children_to_funerals%20(3).pdf, accessed on 21 March 2016.

Elliott, R. (2015) *Missing Jack.* Oxford: Lion Children's Books.

Griffiths, G. and Macleod, L. (2010) *Goodbye Baby: Cameron's Story.* Edinburgh: St Andrew Press.

Jay, C. and Thomas, J. (2012) *What Does Dead Mean? A Book for Young Children to Help Explain Death and Dying.* London: Jessica Kingsley Publishers.

Jeffs, S. (2005) *Rosie: Coming to Terms with the Death of a Sibling.* Abingdon: BRF.

Jeffs, S. (2006) *Josh: Coming to Terms with the Death of a Friend.* Nashville, TN: Abingdon Press.

Kerr, J. (2002) *Goodbye Mog.* London: Collins.

Leutner, D. and Postgate, D. (2009) *Remembering.* Saunderton: Child Bereavement Charity. Available from www.childbereavementuk.org.

Robinson, H. and Straky, M. (2014) *The Cooper Tree.* London: Strauss House Publishers.

Rosen, M. and Blake, Q. (2004) *The Sad Book.* London: Walker.

Sanford, D. and Evans, G. (2014) *It Must Hurt a Lot: A Child's Book about Death* (Hurts of Childhood). London: Random House.

Stickney, D. (2004) *Water Bugs and Dragonflies: Explaining Death to Young Children*. Cleveland, OH: Pilgrim Press.

Thomas, P. (2009) *A First Look at Death: I Miss You*. London: Wayland.

Varley, S. (1985, 1992) *Badger's Parting Gifts*. London: Picture Lions.

Viorst, J. (1971, 1988) *The Tenth Good Thing about Barney*. New York: Aladdin Paperbacks.

Key Stage 2 (seven to eleven years)

Burnett, F.H. (2015) *The Secret Garden*. London: Puffin.

Butler, H. (2013) *Helping Children Think about Bereavement*. London and New York: Routledge, Taylor and Francis.

Erlbruch, W. (2014) *Death, Duck and the Tulip*. Wellington: Gecko Press.

Hughes, S. (2013) *Dealing with Loss: A Workbook for Kids*. Raleigh, NC: Lulu Press.

Leutner, D. and Postgate, D. (2009) *Remembering*, Saunderton: Child Bereavement Charity. Available from www.childbereavementuk.org.

Ness, P. (2011) *A Monster Calls*. London: Walker.

Robinson, H. and Straky, M. (2014) *The Cooper Tree*. London: Strauss House Publishers.

Silverstein, S. (1964) *The Giving Tree*. London: Harper and Row.

Smid, E. (2015) *Luna's Red Hat: An Illustrated Storybook to Help Children Cope with Loss and Suicide*. London: Jessica Kingsley Publishers.

Winston's Wish (2000) *Muddles, Puddles and Sunshine: Your Activity Book to Help when Someone Has Died*. Gloucester: Winston's Wish.

Key Stage 3 (11–14 years)

Boyne, J. (2006) *The Boy in the Striped Pyjamas*. London: Random House.

Magorian, M. (2004) *Goodnight Mister Tom*. London: Penguin.

Mood, P. and Whittaker, L. (2001) *Finding a Way Through When Someone Close has Died: What it Feels Like and What You Can Do to Help Yourself: A Workbook by Young People for Young People*. London: Jessica Kingsley Publishers.

Paterson, K. (1977, 2008) *Bridge to Terabithia*. London: Penguin.

Key Stage 4 (14–16 years)

Hughes, S. (2013) *Dealing with Loss: A Workbook for Kids*. Raleigh, NC: Lulu Press.

Mood, P. and Whittaker, L. (2001) *Finding a Way Through When Someone Close has Died: What it Feels Like and What You Can Do to Help Yourself: A Workbook by Young People for Young People*. London: Jessica Kingsley Publishers.

Pratchett, T. (1991) *Reaper Man*. London: Corgi.

Books for parents and professionals

Bell, J.L. (2005) *The Love Which Heals: A Service of Grieving and Gratitude for those who Have Lost Someone* (2nd ed). Glasgow: Wild Goose Publications.

Cameron, J. (1995) *The Artist's Way: A Course in Discovering and Recovering Your Creative Self*. London: Pan Macmillan.

Collins, M. (2005) *'It's OK to be Sad: Activities to Help Children Aged 4–9 Manage Loss, Grief and Bereavement*. London: Sage Publications.

Dignity Caring Funeral Services (n.d.) *A Child's Questions About Death*. Sutton Coldfield: Dignity Funeral Ltd.

Doughty, C. (2015) *Smoke Gets in Your Eyes: And Other Lessons from the Crematorium*. Edinburgh: Canongate.

Dougy Center, The: The National Center for Grieving Children and Families (2008) *Helping the Grieving Student: A Guide for Teachers*. Portland, OR: The Dougy Center.

Holland, J. (2001) *Understanding Children's Experiences of Parental Bereavement.* London: Jessica Kingsley Publishers.

Holland, J., Dance, R., MacManus, N. and Stitt, C. (2005) *Lost for Words: Loss and Bereavement Awareness Training.* London: Jessica Kingsley Publishers.

Mundy, M. (2009) *What Happens When Someone Dies? A Child's Guide to Death and Funerals.* Meinrad: Abbey Press.

Nash, P. (2011) *Supporting Dying Children and their Families: A Handbook for Christian Ministry.* London: SPCK.

NICE Clinical Guidelines (2015) *Depression in Children and Young People: Identification and Management in Primary Community and Secondary Care.* Available at www.nice.org.uk/guidance/cg28, accessed on 21 March 2016.

Payne, S., Horn, S. and Relf, M. (1999) *Loss and Bereavement.* Buckingham: Open University Press.

Solomon, S., Greenberg, J. and Pyszczynski, T. (2015) *The Worm at the Core: On the Role of Death in Life.* London and New York: Random House.

Stanford, P. (ed.) (2011) *The Death of a Child.* London: Bloomsbury.

Tallis, R. (2015) *The Black Mirror: Fragments of an Obituary for Life.* New Haven, CT: Yale University Press.

Weymont, D. and Rae, T. (2006) *Supporting Young People Coping with Grief, Loss and Death.* London: Sage Publications.

Useful Websites and Organisations

Alliance of Hope for Suicide Survivors

www.allianceofhope.org

A US website offering worldwide support for those affected by suicide.

Bereaved Parents of the USA

www.bereavedparentsusa.org

A US organisation that holds monthly support meetings and produces a newsletter and brochures.

Brake

www.brake.org.uk

A road safety charity for anyone bereaved as a result of a road crash.

Care for the Family

www.careforthefamily.org.uk/family-life/bereavement-support

A faith-based organisation in origin, now offering help to families of faith and none.

Childhood Bereavement Network

www.childhoodbereavementnetwork.org.uk

A comprehensive list of website providers and articles concerning bereavement in children and adolescents. Counselling 14 year olds +.

Child Bereavement UK

www.childbereavement.org.uk

Supports families and professionals when a child dies or when a child is bereaved of someone important in their lives.

Child Death Helpline

www.childdeathhelpline.org.uk

For anyone affected by the death of a child from pre-birth to the death of an adult child. Started by experienced and trained bereaved parent volunteers.

Cruse Bereavement Care

www.cruse.org.uk

Promotes one-to-one support to anyone bereaved and gives information and contact details of local groups. For adolescents help see http// hopeagain.org.uk.

Cruse Bereavement Care Scotland

www.crusescotland.org.uk

Provide the UK services (see above) in Scotland.

CRY (Cardiac Risk in the Young)

www.c-f-y.org.uk

Supports those bereaved through young sudden cardiac death (aged 14–35). CRY promotes heart screening and ECG testing programmes and funds the CRY Centre of Sports Cardiology and Cardiac Pathology. A downloadble booklet for a father losing a child suddenly can be found at www.crydadsgrief.org.

Dying Matters

www.dyingmatters.org

Produces resources and advocates for openness about death.

Gingerbread

www.gingerbread.org.uk

Produces fact sheets and information for single parents following a bereavement.

Grief Encounter

www.griefencounter.com

Grief Encounter is an organisation supporting professionals in helping bereaved children and adolescents in particular school teachers.

Jigsaw4u

www.jigsaw4u.org.uk

A charity helping children/young people put the pieces back together following trauma, loss and bereavement.

MindEd Trust

www.minded.org.uk

Provides help and advice around suicide and young people.

Miscarriage Association

www.miscarriageassociation.org.uk

Supports those who have been affected by the loss of a baby in pregnancy.

Nelsons Journey

www.nelsonsjourney.org.uk

Offers telephone support and guidance, one-to-one therapeutic support and activity days to children and adolescents in Norfolk suffering a significant loss.

NHS

www.nhs.uk/Livewell/bereavement/Pages/children

A useful website giving references to other sources.

Patient Plus

www.patient.info/patientplus

Articles in Patient Plus are written by UK doctors and are based on research evidence and UK and European Guidelines.

SAMM (Support after Murder and Manslaughter)

www.samm.org.uk

Supports those who have been bereaved as a result of murder or manslaughter; information and other activities, including local groups

SANDS (Stillbirth and Neonatal Death Charity)

www.uk-sands.org

Offers support when a baby dies during pregnancy or after birth.

Save the Parents

www.youngminds.org.uk/for_parents/save_the_the_parents_helpline

A site to help parents concerned about the mental health of their children and young people.

Saying Goodbye

www.sayinggoodbye.org

Cathedrals organising memorial services for those who have experienced miscarriage or early loss.

SOBS (Survivors of Bereavement by Suicide)

http://uk-sobs.org.uk

Support for those bereaved by the suicide of a relative or close friend. Information, activities including local groups and events throughout the UK.

The Compassionate Friends

www.tcf.org.uk

Organisation of bereaved parents and their families offering understanding, support and encouragement to others after the death of a child.

Well at School

www.wellatschool.org

Supports children and young people at school with medical and mental health conditions such as depression and self-harm. It produces resources for use in schools.

Winston's Wish

www.winstonswish.org.uk

The organisation exists to support bereaved children and help them make sense of death and rebuild their lives. It produces excellent material for children and adults.

YoungMinds

www.youngminds.org.uk

For parents worried about children/adolescents; improving emotional wellbeing and mental health of children and young people – also offers online support to parents and professionals.

Subject Index

Author Index